CW00816488

Chinese GCSE

中学汉语
Student's Book Vol.2

主 编 李晓琪　副主编 罗青松
编 者 王淑红 刘晓雨 宣 雅

华语教学出版社·伦敦
Sinolingua · London

Every effort has been made to trace all copyright holders, but if any have been inadvertently overlooked, the publisher will be pleased to make the necessary arrangements at the first opportunity.

Chinese GCSE (Student's Book Vol. 2)

Compiler-in-chief: Xiaoqi LI
Deputy compiler-in-chief: Qingsong LUO
Compilers: Shuhong WANG, Xiaoyu LIU, Ya XUAN

Adviser: Xiaoming ZHANG
Consultant editors: Hongxia DU, Jingjing ZHAO, Lu LIN

Editors: Shurong ZHAI, Ranran DU
Cover design: Gu Shou
Layout/Illustration: St.Reach
www.mynicebook.com

Copyright ©2012 by Sinolingua London Ltd.
First published in Great Britain in February 2012 by Sinolingua London Ltd.
Unit 13, Park Royal Metro Centre
Britannia Way
London NW10 7PA
Tel: +44(0)2089519305
Fax: +44(0)2084530709
Email: editor@cypressbooks.com
Website: www.sinolingua.com.cn

Distributed by Cypress Book Co., (UK) Ltd.
Tel: +44(0)2084530687
Fax: +44(0)2084530709
Email: sales@cypressbooks.com
Website: www.cypressbooks.com

Printed in China

ISBN 978-1-907838-03-3

编写说明

《中学汉语》是为以英语为母语的11-16岁中学生编写的汉语教材，全套教材分为三个等级（第一册、第二册和第三册）九本书，每个等级包括学生用书（课本）、教师用书和练习册。全套教材还配有字词卡片、挂图以及CD-ROM、PPT课件等多媒体产品。每册教材可使用一学年（参考学时为90-100学时），全套教材可以供三个年级使用。

一、设计框架

《中学汉语》采用了以新版GCSE大纲交际话题为主线，以语言项目为核心，以文化内容为基本要素的综合性构架，力求做到设计理念与时俱进，语言知识扎实科学，文化内涵丰富生动。

1. 以话题为主线

教材每册有八个单元，每个单元由相关话题的三篇课文组成。每册教材都基本涵盖了Edexcel新版GCSE、AQA中文大纲的主要话题的相关内容，并参照了Asset Language的语言学习要求。教材围绕话题主线，针对不同等级，在语言形式、文化内容上逐步拓展丰富。这种编排方式使学习者无论选取任何阶段的教材，都可较全面地接触新版GCSE大纲的交际话题，从而在提高交际能力，以及准备考试方面得到帮助。如：初学者可以在学完第一、二册后，参加GCSE考试，第三册则用于巩固提高，并逐步向AS过渡。而具备一定汉语基础的学生，也可以直接从第二册或第三册开始学习。

2. 以语言项目为核心

教材以新版GCSE大纲提供的560个核心词语和85个语法项目为教材内容的重点与核心，全套教材覆盖了新大纲的全部语言项目——词汇和语言点。此外，还根据日常交际需要，以及教学对象、学习环境的特点，进行了合理调整与拓展，以达到在控制教材难度的基础上，丰富教材内容，满足话题表达需求的目的。教材各等级语言项目分布如下：

第一册：汉字145个左右，生词237个，句型91个。

第二册：汉字150个左右，生词233个，句型93个。

第三册：汉字160个左右，生词230个，句型95个。

书中句型除了在新版大纲基础上进行拓展之外，编写组还从教材语言点设置与编排的科学性与实用性出发，将新版大纲中概括表述的句型具体化，并进行合理分级。如在新版GCSE中文大纲中，情态动词只作为一个语言点给出，用"他会说普通话"概括这一语言形式，我们在教材中处理为"他能说普通话"、"你应该学习中文"等多个语言点。这样不仅更全面地表现出情态动词的特点，也便于在教学中分解难点，科学、合理、有序、全面地安排教学内容。

3. 以文化内容为基本要素

《中学汉语》注重文化内容，并将其与语言学习目标、教学对象与教学环境结合起来加以体现。本套教材的文化内容反映在话题设计、课文内容、练习设计、画面展示、教学提示等方面，以期逐步培养学习者的目的文化意识，拓展他们的文化视野；而通过教材丰富多样的文化体现，也可进一步增强教材的知识性与趣味性。

二、教材结构

1. 学生用书

学生用书是教材的核心。每课的基本版块有学习目标提示、课文、词语以及听说读写译练习。学生用书上的练习作为课堂操练使用，主要围绕教学目标，从听说读写译几个方面进行操练。每三课为一个单元，每个单元后有句型小结，帮助学生总结语言知识；同时，还设置了与单元话题相关的文化，以增进学生对中国文化的感性认识。学生用书的编写原则是简明、适用，符合课堂教学需要，同时又注重效果，循序渐进地增进学生的语言技能与文化认知。

2. 教师用书

教师用书的主要作用是帮助教师较为便捷地在内容、方法上进行教学准备。每课的基本版块有：教学内容提示、教学步骤与建议、练习参考答案、相关语言知识点和文化背景知识的简要说明，此外，还根据教学需要，提供了一些课堂活动和小游戏。每个单元提供了一套单元测验题，考题设计综合了单元学习内容，形式上也逐步靠近GCSE考试题型。教师在教学中可用于考查学生阶段学习情况，从而循序渐进地帮助学生适应考试，最终达到GCSE考试的标准。

3. 练习册

练习册为教材提供外围的辅助练习，练习安排与学生用书中的练习相辅相成，作为课堂练习的拓展，供学习者课下使用，或用来丰富课堂训练项目。提供多样化的练习，可以进一步充实课堂教学的内容；提供有选择的练习，也可以让学生有机会自主学习，增强自学能力。

4. 其他配套资源

为方便使用者，本套教材还有生词卡片、多媒体材料等，增加教与学的互动性和生动性，方便师生课堂教学和自学。

三、教材特色

《中学汉语》关注教学对象的特点，注重使用者的基本目的和要求，教材的突出特点表现为以下几个方面。

1. 针对性与目的性统一

本套教材针对中学阶段的英语为母语的汉语学习者编写。通过本套教材的学习，学生可全面提高汉语交际能力，并在听说读写技能上全面达到GCSE中文考试大纲的标准和要求。

2. 全面性与基础性统一

本套教材在话题、语音、汉字、词汇、句型、文化等方面，全面覆盖新版GCSE中文考试大纲的内容；同时，根据学生水平等级、交际需要及汉语本身的特点进行全面规划，合理增补，科学编排。同时，教材设计也充分考虑到中学生汉语学习的基本目标与认知特点，突出基础知识、基本技能的掌握，注重内容编排难度、容量、梯级的合理性。

3．科学性与趣味性统一

教材针对教学对象的特点，体现寓教于乐的编写理念。话题贴近学生现实生活，生活场景的设置真实自然，课文内容自然活泼，练习形式丰富多样，注重实用性和互动性。此外，教材还通过图文并茂的文化介绍，拓展学生文化视野，增强教材的趣味性，从而使得学习者获得有趣、有用的汉语学习体验。

为此套教材的策划和出版，华语教学出版社的王君校社长、韩晖总编和伦敦分社的茹静总经理，以及责任编辑翟淑蓉、杜然然付出了大量的心血，对此我们表示衷心的感谢；此外英国的张小明、杜宏霞、赵晶晶、林璐四位老师和梁乔、何晓红、吴允红、黄珍理等诸位一线教师的积极参与，为本教材的问世给予了很大的帮助，我们编写组的全体成员对你们也说一声：谢谢！

设计一套全面系统的针对性教材，是一项有挑战性的工作，需要长期努力。我们的错误和疏漏在所难免，期望各位同仁提出宝贵意见，我们将不断完善，使《中学汉语》更好地为课堂教学提供帮助。

《中学汉语》编写组

Compilers' Words

Chinese GCSE is designed for secondary school students in English speaking countries who are aged from 11-16. This three-volume series covers three levels. Each level includes a student's book, a workbook, a teacher's book, Chinese character flash cards, wall charts, and multimedia support through CD-ROMs and PowerPoint courseware. Each volume corresponds to one academic year (90-100 class hours) and the whole series can be used consecutively over three grades.

Design Framework

Chinese GCSE is organized according to the new GCSE syllabus with a topic-oriented structure that takes the language as its core and the cultural content as its key element. The series is thus designed as a full set of materials, which includes both comprehensive language knowledge and enriched cultural content.

1. Key Topics

The series covers all the areas in the new Edexcel Chinese GCSE and AQA syllabus, and takes the Asset Language requirements as its reference. Each volume has eight units, with each unit containing three lessons that focus on one topic or activity. The vocabulary and grammar develop step by step so that students can familiarise themselves with new topics covered by the Chinese GCSE, while simultaneously developing their conversational skills as they prepare for the exam. Beginners may take the GCSE exam after completing the first two volumes, and then take the third volume as a preparatory guide for the AS exam. Those who have a certain command of the Chinese language may start from either volume 2 or 3.

2. Language as the Core

The series covers all the 560 core words and 85 grammar points required by the new Chinese GCSE syllabus. On top of this, the contents have been organized and extended to satisfy the daily communicative needs of the learners, while also ensuring the inclusion of extensive extra content and expressions, all of which are based on the Chinese GCSE course requirements. The language points are arranged as follows:

Volume 1: 145 Chinese characters, 237 new words, 91 sentence patterns

Volume 2: 150 Chinese characters, 233 new words, 93 sentence patterns

Volume 3: 160 Chinese characters, 230 new words, 95 sentence patterns

The sentence patterns have been extended based on the new Chinese GCSE syllabus, and have been substantiated and sequenced according to their level of difficulty. For example, in the new Chinese GCSE syllabus, the modal verb is given as a language point and expressed in the sentence 他会说普通话. However, in this series we have modified that entry into several language points, such as 他能说普通话, 你应该学习中文, etc. This more fully displays the characteristics of modal verbs, helps to ease learning difficulties, and provides a better organization and format of instruction.

3. Cultural Contents as the Key Elements

Chinese GCSE places an emphasis on cultural information, which is combined with language objectives and methods of teaching to provide a nurturing learning environment. As shown in the topics, texts, exercises, pictures and teaching tips of the series, the cultural contents are aimed at cultivating students' cultural consciousness and extending their cultural vision. This diversified cultural content renders the books more interesting and informative to students, which in turn makes them a more effective learning tool.

Structure of the Series

1. Student's Book

The Student's Book is the core book of the series. Each lesson consists of sections such as learning objectives, text, new words, and exercises for listening, speaking, reading, writing and translating which can be used as practical exercises in class. Three lessons form a unit, followed by a unit summary which reviews the language points of the lessons, and also includes cultural tips for a more comprehensive understanding of Chinese. The Student's Book is both concise and practical, and aims to develop the language learning skills and cultural recognition of the students in a gradual manner.

2. Teacher's Book

The Teacher's Book pedagogically prepares the instructors to teach the series' contents in a fun and nurturing learning environment. Each lesson includes teaching suggestions, keys to the exercises, and additional cultural information. Furthermore, it provides a number of suggestions for classroom activities and games. A test is provided after each unit based on its content, and is close to the GCSE test in format. This test can serve as a tool to gauge the students' progress, and further prepare them for the GCSE exams.

3. Workbook

This includes exercises as a complement to the Student's Book. As an extension of classroom exercises, it may be used both in class and at home. These exercises not only supplement classroom teaching, but also provide materials for self study and a chance for the students to improve their language abilities outside of class.

4. Additional Resources

The series also provides illustrations of commonly used words, flash cards, and multimedia software to increase the convenience of teaching and self study, making both the teaching and studying of this series a more interactive and dynamic process.

Features

This series has been closely tailored to meet students' basic objectives and studying needs. This has been done through the following:

1. Having an Aligned Focus

The target readers of the series are secondary school Chinese language students whose native language is English. Through their study, students can fully improve their communicative ability in Chinese, and reach the standard required to successfully sit the Chinese GCSE exam in listening, speaking, and reading and writing skills.

2. Fully Integrating Basic Language Knowledge

This series covers all the requirements of the new Chinese GCSE syllabus in its topics, phonetics, characters, vocabularies, sentences, cultural knowledge, etc. It is clearly organized into different levels of language ability and knowledge, social settings and characteristics of the Chinese language. The objectives and recognition patterns of secondary school students have been fully taken into consideration. It emphasizes cementing a solid command, as well as introducing students to more difficult and advanced language points to encourage further study.

3. Being Practical and Fun to Use

The topics covered relate to the students' real lives, and include realistic scenarios; the content is dynamic, and the exercises are diverse, practical and useful. Through illustrated cultural introductions, this series hopes to expand the cultural visions of the students, and as a result of this, we hope the students will in turn have a rewarding experience learning Chinese.

For their help and support during the compilation of this series, we would like to extend our heartfelt thanks to Mr. Wang Junxiao, President of Sinolingua, Ms. Han Hui, Editor-in-chief of Sinolingua, Ms. Ru Jing, Managing Director of Sinolingua London Ltd., as well as Sinolingua editors Zhai Shurong and Du Ranran. Thanks also go to Zhang Xiaoming, Du Hongxia, Zhao Jingjing, Lin Lu and many other teachers in Britain.

It's a challenge to compile a series of textbooks that is both comprehensive and practical, and has clear academic focus. We have thoroughly enjoyed this process of creation and we welcome the opinions and comments of our peers and students alike.

Characters in the Text

大海 中国人
Dàhǎi

小雨 中国人
Xiǎoyǔ

天天 中国人
Tiāntiān

京京 中国人
Jīngjīng

Characters in the Text

大卫 David 英国人
Dàwèi

玛丽 Mary 英国人
Mǎlì

本 Ben 英国人
Běn

丽丽 Lily 英国人
Lìli

月份
yuèfèn
Month

一月 yī yuè January	二月 èr yuè February	三月 sān yuè March	四月 sì yuè April
五月 wǔ yuè May	六月 liù yuè June	七月 qī yuè July	八月 bā yuè August
九月 jiǔ yuè September	十月 shí yuè October	十一月 shíyī yuè November	十二月 shí'er yuè December

季节
jìjié
The Four Seasons

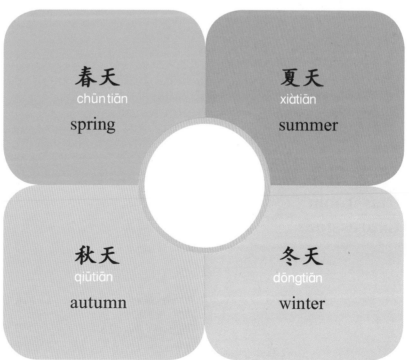

春天
chūn tiān
spring

夏天
xiàtiān
summer

秋天
qiūtiān
autumn

冬天
dōngtiān
winter

社交用语
Social Greetings

Hello.	你好。
Hello, everyone.	大家好。
Good evening.	晚上好。
Good night.	晚安。
Goodbye.	再见。
See you tomorrow.	明天见。
Excuse me.	请问。
Thank you.	谢谢。
Sorry.	对不起。
It doesn't matter.	没关系。

课堂用语
Classroom Expressions

Good morning.	早上好。
Hello, Miss/Sir.	老师好。
Hello, everyone.	同学们好。
It's time for class.	现在上课。
Read after me.	跟我读。
Once again, please.	再说一遍。
Time for break.	休息一会儿。
Class is over.	现在下课。

目 录
CONTENTS

第一课 Lesson

1

Do You Know His Phone Number?
你知道他的电话吗？

Learning Objectives

交际话题 **Topic of conversation:**
联系方式
Liánxì fāngshì
Information and Contact Details

基本句型 **Sentence patterns:**
你姓什么？叫什么名字？
我姓周，叫周英。
他的电话是72840516。
我周末常常在家看书。

New Words

1. 先生 xiānsheng **n.** mister, sir
2. 姓 xìng **v.** to be surnamed; to be called by a surname
3. 张 Zhāng **n./m.w.** (a surname); (a measure word used for tickets, paper and photos)
4. 名字 míngzi **n.** name
5. 周 Zhōu **n.** (a surname)
6. 王 Wáng **n.** (a surname)
7. 电话 diànhuà **n.** telephone
8. 号码 hàomǎ **n.** number
9. 见面 jiànmiàn **v.** to meet
10. 学习 xuéxí **v.** to study, to learn
11. 地方 dìfang **n.** place

— 1

Text

Part I

老师：你好！

大海：您好，先生。
　　　　　　xiānsheng

老师：你是北京人吗？
　　　　Běijīngrén

大海：是的，我是北京人。

老师：你姓什么？
　　　xìng

大海：我姓张。
　　　　Zhāng

老师：你叫什么名字？
　　　　　　　míngzi

大海：我叫张大海。您呢？

老师：我姓周，叫周英。张天海
　　　Zhōu,

　　　先生是你的朋友吗？

大海：是，他是我哥哥。

老师：你知道他在哪儿吗？

大海：他去王老师家了。
　　　　　Wáng

老师：你知道他的电话吗？
　　　　　　　diànhuà

　　　我想和他见面。
　　　　　　　jiànmiàn

大海：他的电话号码是72840516。
　　　　　　　hàomǎ

老师：谢谢你。

Part II

我是中文老师

我姓周，周末的周，我叫周英。我是中文老师，有很多学生。我有英国

学生、法国学生和美国学生。他们都不是中国人，他们都在北京学习。我的学
xuéxí

生都有好听的中文名字，他们都喜欢自己的中文名字。北京有很多有意思的

地方，学生们常常去玩。我喜欢看书，我周末常常在家看书。
dìfang

Exercises

Read 1 *Read the following words and then match them with the proper pictures.*

A 姓名　　B 电话　　C 号码　　D 上学　　E 地方
F 先生　　G 朋友　　H 老师　　I 看书　　J 玩

F　　　　B　　　　E　　　　H　　　　C

J　　　　G　　　　I　　　　A　　　　D

Listen 2 *Listen to the recording and then choose the correct answer.*

1) 你＿＿姓生＿＿什么？　　　　A 姓　　　　B 叫

2) 你叫什么＿名字＿？　　　　　A 姓名　　　B 名字

3) 你知道他的＿电话＿吗？　　　A 名字　　　B 电话

4) 张＿先生＿是您的朋友吗？　　A 同学　　　B 先生

5) 我哥哥在北京＿学习＿。　　　A 学习　　　B 旅行

Listen 3 *Listen to the recording and then tick the correct box.*

A	B	C	D	E	F
Zhang Dahai	85673240	Zhou Ying	lives in Beijing, China	reads at home during the weekends	studies in Shanghai

	A	B	C	D	E	F
大海	✓					
小雨				✓		
王老师的电话号码		✓				
中文老师的名字			✓			
天天						✓
玛丽				✓		

Read 4 *Read the following sentences and then match them with the proper pictures.*

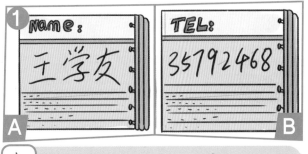

A 你姓什么？叫什么名字？

A 我姓周，叫周英。

B 你知道他的电话吗？

A 张先生的电话是010-84567899

⬜ 我有一个中文名字。

⬜ 老师有很多中国学生。

⬜ 我周末常常在家看书。

⬜ 我的家在北京。

Read 5 *Read the following paragraph and answer the questions below in Chinese.*

　　我是法国的女学生，我喜欢中文，每个周末我都上中文课。我有一个中文名字，姓王，叫王天安，天安门的天安。我的老师姓周，叫周英，周末的周，英国的英。他是中国人，他家在北京。我们都喜欢他的中文课。

Questions:

1) *Does she have a Chinese name? What's her Chinese name?*

　　she has a chinese name, it is wangtian'an

2) *Which country is Tian'an from?*

　　France

3) *Who is Tian'an's Chinese teacher?*

　　Mr Zhou

4) *Where is Mr Zhou from?*

　　China

Write 6 *Complete the sentences with the proper Chinese characters.*

1) 我 姓 (xìng) 张，我叫张大海。

2) 我没有中文 名 字 (míngzi)。

3）您知道他的   (diànhuà) 号码吗？

4）你家在什么   (dìfang)？在北京吗？

5）周末我哥哥要和他的同学   (jiànmiàn)。

Talk 7　*Talk about the pictures in Chinese.*

Talk 8　*Answer the following questions in Chinese.*

1）What's Dahai's elder brother's name?

2）What's Dahai's elder brother's telephone number?

3）What's the occupation of Zhou Ying?

4）Where are Zhou Ying's students from?

5）Where is Zhou Ying from?

6）What does Zhou Ying do on the weekends?

7）What do the students do on the weekends?

Write
9

Write the following Chinese characters.

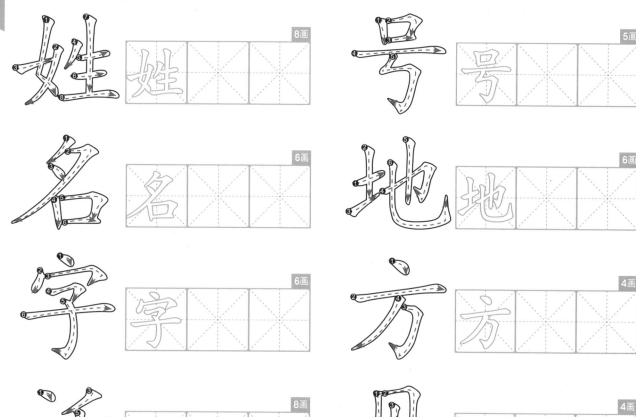

Read
10

Phonetics.

歌谣(A Rhyme)
Gēyáo

我和你
Wǒ hé nǐ

我和你，心连心，同住地球村；
Wǒ hé nǐ， xīn lián xīn， tóng zhù dìqiúcūn；

为梦想，千里行，相会在北京。
wèi mèngxiǎng， qiān lǐ xíng， xiāng huì zài Běijīng。

第二课 *Lesson* **2**

We Often Chat Online 我们常常在网上聊天儿

Learning Objectives

交际话题 Topic of conversation:
网络联系 Online Contacts
Wǎngluò liánxì

基本句型 Sentence patterns:
他们周末在网上聊天儿。
他们常常写信吗?
我给哥哥发电子邮件。

New Words

1 学校 xuéxiào **n.** school
2 教书 jiāo shū **v.** to teach
3 写 xiě **v.** to write
4 信 xìn **n.** letter
5 上 shàng **prep/v.** on; to go up; to serve
6 聊天儿 liáo tiānr **v.** to chat
7 发 fā **v.** to send; to hand out
8 电子邮件 diànzǐ yóujiàn **n.** e-mail
9 认识 rènshi **v.** to know
10 给 gěi **v./prep.** to give, to let; to, for
11 介绍 jièshào **v.** to introduce
12 小学 xiǎoxué **n.** primary school
13 用 yòng **v.** to use

Text

Part I

（大海在英国的家中和本聊天儿）

本：　　周英是你的朋友吗？

大海：　不是，他是我哥哥的朋友。

　　　　他在学校教书，他是中文老师。
　　　　　 xuéxiào jiāo shū

本：　　他的学校在哪儿？

大海：　他的学校在北京。

本：　　他和你哥哥常常见面吗？

大海：　不，我哥哥在伦敦工作，

　　　　周英在北京工作。

本：　　他们常常写信吗？
　　　　　　　 xiě xìn

大海：　不，他们周末在网上聊天儿，
　　　　　　　　　　　 wǎng shàng liáo tiānr

　　　　也发电子邮件。
　　　　 fā diànzǐ yóujiàn

本：　　我爸爸打算八月去北京工作，

我和妈妈想一起去，我想认识
　　　　　　　　　　　　 rènshi
周英，在他的班上学习中文。

大海：　我给哥哥发电子邮件，介绍
　　　　 gěi 　　　　　　　 jièshào
你们认识。

Part II

我在北京学中文

我在北京的学校学习中文，我的中文老师叫周英，他是中国人。他有

一个弟弟叫周华，在伦敦的小学学习。他们常常在网上聊天儿。周华也是
Zhōu Huá　　　　　xiǎoxué

我的朋友，我常常给他写电子邮件，他也常常给我写电子邮件。我们用英
yòng

文写，也用中文写。我们也喜欢在电话上聊天儿，我们常常聊北京，也聊

伦敦。

Exercises

Read
1 Read the following words and then match them with the proper pictures.

A 学校　　B 教书　　C 在网上　　D 电子邮件　　E 聊天儿
F 写　　　G 信　　　H 看新闻　　I 听音乐　　　　J 玩电子游戏

....　.............　.............　.............　.............

....　.............　.............　.............　.............

Listen
2 Listen to the recording and then choose the correct answer.

1）周英在＿＿＿A＿＿＿教书。　　　A 中学　　　B 小学

2）我们都会＿＿＿B＿＿＿电子邮件。　A 用　　　　B 发

3）我常常给他写＿＿＿B＿＿＿。　　　A 信　　　　B 电子邮件

4）我们周末常常上网＿＿A＿＿。　　　A 聊天儿　　B 听音乐

5）他弟弟在伦敦＿＿B＿＿英文。　　　A 教　　　　B 学

Listen 3 *Listen to the recording and then tick the correct box.*

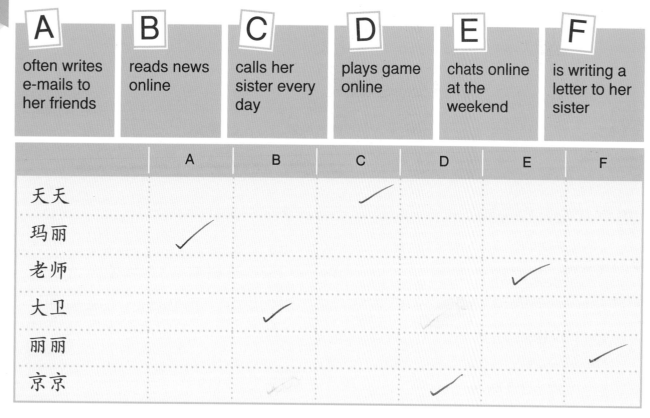

A	often writes e-mails to her friends
B	reads news online
C	calls her sister every day
D	plays game online
E	chats online at the weekend
F	is writing a letter to her sister

	A	B	C	D	E	F
天天			✓			
玛丽	✓					
老师					✓	
大卫		✓				
丽丽						✓
京京				✓		

Read 4 *Read the following sentences and then match them with the proper pictures.*

A 我哥哥在小学教书。

B 她喜欢用电话聊天儿。

B 我在网上发电子邮件。

B 请给我写信。

A 弟弟常常在网上玩电子游戏。

B 弟弟在伦敦上学。

Read
5 *Read the following paragraph and answer the questions below in Chinese.*

我叫小雨，是中学生。我家在北京，我现在在伦敦上学。今天是周末，我没有课。我在家上网。我给爷爷、奶奶写电子邮件。我有很多朋友，他们都在北京。我们常常在网上聊天儿。我也在网上看新闻、听音乐。我很喜欢上网。

Questions:

1) *Where is Xiaoyu from?*

...........Beijing...

2) *Where does Xiaoyu study?*

...........London...

3) *Does Xiaoyu have lessons today?*

...........No...

4) *What does Xiaoyu do on the weekends?*

....

5) *How does Xiaoyu contact her friends?*

....

6) *How does Xiaoyu contact her grandparents?*

....

Write
6 *Complete the sentences with the proper Chinese characters.*

1）我常常在 网 上 (wǎng shàng) 聊天儿。

2）我妈妈喜欢 (jiāo shū) 教 书 。

3）明天是我朋友的生日，我在 给 (gěi) 他 写 信 (xiě xìn)。

4）请给我发 电 子 (diànzǐ) 邮件。

5）他们 用 (yòng) 中文聊天儿。

Talk 7 *Talk about what Tiantian did on the weekends in Chinese according to the pictures.*

Talk 8 Answer the following questions in Chinese.

她给父母打电话。

1）How does Jingjing contact her parents?
2）How does Jingjing contact her friend Xiaoyu?
3）How does Jingjing contact her teacher?
4）How do you contact your friends?
5）How do you contact your classmates?
6）If your parents want to contact your teacher, how do they do?

Write 9 Write the following Chinese characters.

 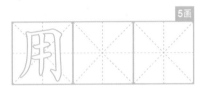　5画

 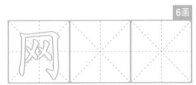　6画

 　9画

 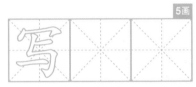　5画

 　9画

 　10画

Read 10 Phonetics.

古诗(A Classical Poem)
Gǔshī

相思
Xiāngsī

唐 · 王维
Táng · Wáng Wéi

红豆生南国，春来发几枝。
Hóngdòu shēng nán guó,　chūn lái fā jǐ zhī.

愿君多采撷，此物最相思。
Yuàn jūn duō cǎixié,　cǐ wù zuì xiāngsī.

第三课 **Lesson**

How Old Are You? 你多大?

3

Learning Objectives

交际话题 Topic of conversation:

朋友信息 Friends' Information
Péngyou xìnxī

基本句型 Sentence patterns:

你多大?

我今年16岁。

他的个子高吗?

他会说汉语吗?

他比我高。

New Words

1 多大 duō dà   how old

2 今年 jīnnián   n. this year

3 岁 suì   n./m.w. year of age; years old

4 英语 Yīngyǔ   n. English

5 个子 gèzi   n. height

6 高 gāo   adj./n. tall; (a person's) height

7 比 bǐ   prep. than; compared with

8 去年 qùnián   n. last year

9 说 shuō   v. to speak, to talk

10 汉语 Hànyǔ   n. Chinese

11 外语 wàiyǔ   n. foreign language

12 法语 Fǎyǔ   n. French

Text

Part I

丽丽：京京，你多大？
　　　　　　duō dà

京京：我今年16岁。
　　　jīnnián　suì

丽丽：大海是你的同学吗?

京京：他是我英语班的同学。
　　　　　　Yīngyǔ

丽丽：他今年多大?

京京：他今年也是16岁。

丽丽：他的个子高吗?
　　　　　gèzi gāo

京京：他比我高。去年我比他高。
　　　　bǐ　　　qùnián

丽丽：他会说汉语吗?
　　　　shuō Hànyǔ

京京：他会说汉语。他说得不

好，他哥哥说得比他好。

丽丽：天天也是中国人，也是你的
　　　朋友吧?

京京：是的，他是我的朋友，他比
　　　我大。

丽丽：他多大?

京京：他今年17岁。

Part II

他们都会说外语
wàiyǔ

　　京京和大海是同学，也是好朋友，他们都会说汉语。现在他们一起在英国学习，他们也会说英语。京京和大海今年都是16岁，大海比京京高。飞飞不是他们的同学，他是京京的朋友，他18岁，他比京京大。他学法语，他的法语
　　　　　　　　　　　　　　　　　　　　　　　　　　　　　　　　　　　Fǎyǔ
说得很好。八月学校放暑假，他们想一起去旅行，先去法国，再去美国。

Exercises

Read 1 *Match the English with the Chinese.*

A 多大   B 比   C 说汉语   D 个子高
E 喜欢旅行   F 会说法语   G 小个子   H 写英语

to speak French	how old	than	to enjoy travelling
F	A	B	E

tall	can speak Chinese	to write English	short
D	C	H	G

Listen 2 *Listen to the recording and then choose the correct answer.*

1) 我＿＿＿B＿＿＿16岁。   A 今年   B 去年

2) 他是我＿＿＿B＿＿＿课的同学。   A 法语   B 英语

3) 大海比我＿＿＿A＿＿＿。   A 高   B 小

4) 天天会＿＿＿A＿＿＿法语。   A 说   B 听

5) 我的朋友比我＿＿＿A＿＿＿。   A 大   B 小

Listen 3 *Listen to the recording and then tick the correct box.*

A	B	C	D	E	F
is 17 this year	is taller than her sister	thinks classical music is better than pop music	is 11 this year	can speak Chinese	travelled to China last year

	A	B	C	D	E	F
天天	✓					

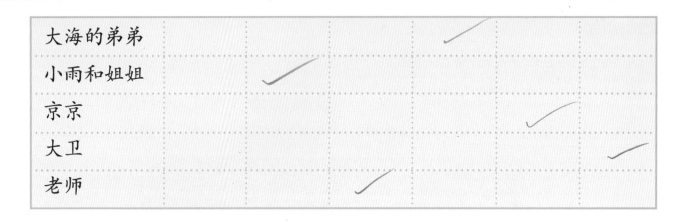

大海的弟弟

小雨和姐姐

京京

大卫

老师

Read 4 *Complete the sentences according to the pictures.*

1　天天比京京 大 。

A 大　　B 小

2　12月北京比香港 冷 。

A 热　　B 冷

3　妹妹比我 高 。

A 高　　B 大

4　这本书比那本书＿＿＿＿。

A 没兴趣　B 有意思

5　他踢足球踢得比我 好 。

A 好　　B 高

Read 5 *Read the following paragraph and answer the questions below in Chinese.*

　　Lisa今年十五岁，她是中学生，她在香港上学。她喜欢上英语课，她的英语说得很好。Lisa有一个弟弟，他今年十岁，他是小学生。弟弟也会说英语。在香港，小学生也学英语。Lisa比她弟弟高，她的英语比她弟弟的好。早上他们一起去学校。

Questions:

1) How old is Lisa?

15 ✓

2) Where does she study?

Hong Kong ✓

3) Which subject does she like at school?

English ✓

4) Does she speak English?

Yes, she speaks it very well ✓

5) How old is Lisa's younger brother?

10 ✓

6) Who is taller, Lisa or her younger brother?

Lisa ✓

Talk 6 *Talk about the pictures in Chinese.*

1   大卫   京京

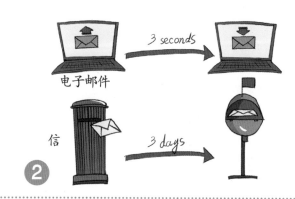

2   电子邮件   3 seconds   信   3 days

3   丽丽   玛丽

4   天天，17岁   京京，16岁

5   弟弟小海   大海

Write 7 *Complete the sentences with the proper Chinese characters.*

1）京京16 岁 (suì)，天天17 岁 (suì)。

2）天天 比 (bǐ) 京京大一岁。

3）今 年 (nián) 你多大？

4）你会 说 (shuō) 英 语 (Yīngyǔ)吗？

5）姐姐比玛丽 高 (gāo)。

Talk 8 *Look at the pictures and answer the following questions in Chinese.*

1）How old is Zhang Ziyi?
2）How old is Yao Ming?
3）Who is the elder one?
4）Who is the taller one?
5）Do they speak English?

姓　　名：姚明（Yao Ming）
生　　日：1980年9月12日
出 生 地：上海
居 住 地：休斯顿、上海
身　　高：226 cm
工　　作：打篮球

姓　　名：章子怡（Zhang Ziyi）
生　　日：1979年2月9日
出 生 地：北京
居 住 地：北京
身　　高：164 cm
工　　作：演电影

Write
9 **Write the following Chinese characters.**

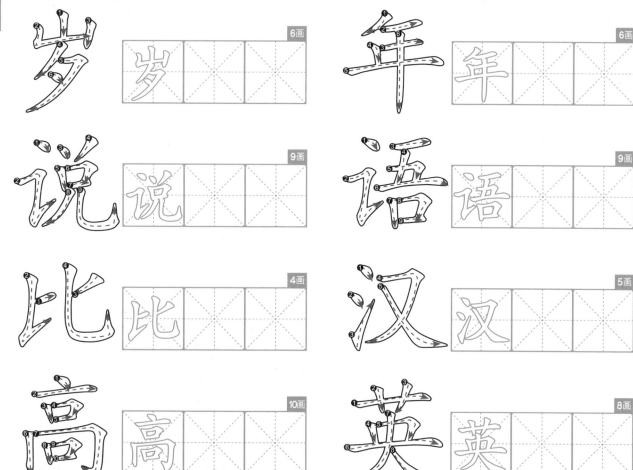

Read
10 *Phonetics.*

歌谣 (A Rhyme)
Gēyáo

小星星
Xiǎo xīngxing

一闪一闪亮晶晶， 满天都是小星星。
Yì shǎn yì shǎn liàngjīngjīng,　　mǎn tiān dōu shì xiǎo xīngxing.

挂在天空放光明， 好像无数小眼睛。
Guà zài tiānkōng fàng guāngmíng,　　hǎoxiàng wúshù xiǎo yǎnjing.

印刷术

　　印刷术是中国古代四大发明之一。它开始于隋朝(公元581-618)的雕版印刷，经宋代(公元960-1279)的毕昇发展、完善，产生了活字印刷，所以后人称毕昇为印刷术的始祖。中国的印刷术为知识的广泛传播、交流创造了条件。印刷术先后传到朝鲜、日本等国，以及中亚、西亚和欧洲等地区。

Printing

Printing is one of the four great inventions of ancient China. Block printing appeared in the Sui Dynasty (581-618), and was the first technique of this kind to be put into use. In the Song Dynasty(960-1279), Bi Sheng renovated this printing technique and invented movable type printing, which boosted printing efficiency. Bi Sheng is regarded as the father of printing. The invention of Chinese printing created favourable conditions for the spread of knowledge and communication. It was gradually introduced into Korea, Japan, Central Asia, Western Asia and Europe.

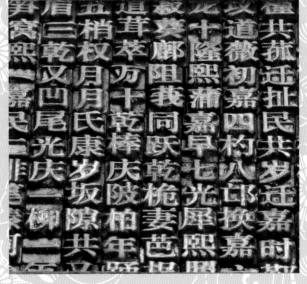

1 某人＋姓＋什么？ Sb. + be surnamed + what? （某人）＋叫＋什么＋名字？ (Sb. +) is + what + full name?	你姓什么？叫什么名字？ What is your surname? What is your full name? 中文老师姓什么？叫什么名字？ What is the Chinese teacher's surname? What is the Chinese teacher's full name?
2 某人＋姓＋中国姓氏，（某人）＋叫＋姓＋名。 Sb. + is + surname, (sb.) + is + family name + given name.	我姓周，叫周英。 My surname is Zhou. My full name is Zhou Ying. 老师姓王，叫王小红。 The teacher's surname is Wang. Her full name is Wang Xiaohong.
3 某人＋的＋电话（号码）＋是＋（××）数字。 Sb.'s + phone number + is + numbers.	他的电话是84076512。 His phone number is 84076512. 王老师的电话号码是8899781。 Teacher Wang's phone number is 8899781.
4 某人＋时间名词（＋常常）＋在＋处所＋动词（＋宾语）。 Sb. + time (+ usually) + at + somewhere + verb (+ object).	我周末常常在图书馆看书。 I usually read books in the library on the weekends. 妈妈晚上常常在家看电视。 Mum usually watches TV at home in the evenings.
5 某人＋在＋网上＋动词（＋宾语）。 Sb. + is + on the Internet + verb (+ object).	我在网上聊天儿。 I'm chatting on the Internet. 哥哥在网上看新闻。 The elder brother is watching the news on the Internet.
6 （某人＋）给＋某人＋动词（＋宾语）。 (Sb. +) to + sb. + verb (+ object).	给他写信。 Write him a letter. 给爸爸、妈妈发电子邮件。 Write an e-mail to Dad and Mum.
7 某人＋多大（了）？ Sb. + how old (了)?	你多大（了）？ How old are you? 弟弟多大（了）？ How old is your younger brother?

第一单元小结 Unit One Summary

8	主语＋多＋形容词？ Subject + how + adjective?	他多高？ How tall is he? 你的房间多大？ How big is your room?
9	某人＋时间（年份）＋年龄。 Sb. + time (year) + age.	我今年16岁。 I'm 16 years old. 他的姐姐今年17岁。 His elder sister is 17 years old.
10	某人＋会＋动词＋宾语。 Sb. + can + verb + object.	他会说英语。 He can speak English. 哥哥会开车。 The elder brother can drive.
11	某人₁/某地₁＋比＋某人₂/某地₂＋ 形容词。 Sb. ₁/somewhere ₁ + compared with + sb. ₂/somewhere ₂ + adjective (comparative).	她比我大。 She is older than me. 北京比香港冷。 Beijing is colder than Hong Kong.

第四课 Lesson **4**

This Is Jingjing's Home 这是京京的家

Learning Objectives

交际话题 Topic of conversation:

房间格局 Room Structures
Fángjiān géjú

基本句型 Sentence patterns:

这就是我的家。
我的卧室在旁边。
厨房在客厅的南边。
卫生间在客厅旁边。

New Words

1 就 jiù **adv.** exactly, precisely
2 真 zhēn **adj./adv.** real; really
3 漂亮 piàoliang **adj.** beautiful
4 客厅 kètīng **n.** living room
5 卧室 wòshì **n.** bedroom
6 厨房 chúfáng **n.** kitchen
7 南 nán **n.** south

8 边 biān **n.** side
9 对面 duìmiàn **n.** the opposite
10 卫生间 wèishēngjiān **n.** bathroom
11 北 běi **n.** north
12 东 dōng **n.** east
13 西 xī **n.** west

Text

Part I

大卫：天天，这是你的家吗？

天天：是的，这就是我的家。
　　　　　　jiù

大卫：你家真漂亮！
　　　zhēn piàoliang

天天：谢谢！

大卫：你家有几个房间？

天天：我家有六个房间，客厅是
　　　　　　　　　　　kètīng
　　　最大的房间。

大卫：这是谁的房间？

天天：这是我爸爸妈妈的卧室。
　　　　　　　　　　wòshì

大卫：你的卧室在哪儿？

天天：我的卧室在旁边。

大卫：厨房在哪儿？
　　　chúfáng

天天：厨房在客厅的南边。
　　　　　　　　　nán

大卫：你姐姐的卧室呢？

天天：她的卧室在我房间的对面。
　　　　　　　　　　　　duìmiàn

大卫：你弟弟的卧室在哪儿？

天天：我的卧室也是弟弟的卧室。

大卫：卫生间呢？
　　　wèishēngjiān

天天：卫生间在客厅旁边。

Part II

京京的家很漂亮

这是京京的家！她家很大，有八个房间。她爸爸妈妈的卧室在南边，
This is jingjing's house! her house inveny big, it has 8 rooms. Her parents bedroom is south

哥哥的卧室在北边，京京自己的卧室在东边，卫生间在爸爸妈妈卧室的西
her older brother's bedroom is north, běi *jingjing's own room is east dōng, the bathroom is west of her parents' bedroom* xī

边。客厅在南边，客厅很大，也很漂亮。周末朋友们喜欢去京京家，他们
the living room is south, her living room is very big, also very beautiful. On weekends friends often like to go to her house, they

在京京家喝茶，听音乐，读书，京京家有很多好看的书。
drink tea in jingjing's house, listen to music, read books, jingjing has many good books to read

Exercises

Read 1 *Read the following words and then match them with the proper pictures.*

A 卫生间   B 卧室   C 客厅   D 东   E 南
F 西   G 北   H 厨房   I 对面   J 漂亮

 J ✓
 A ✓
 G ✓
 H ✓
 C ✓

 I ✓
 D ✓
 F ✓
B ✓
E ✓

Listen 2 *Listen to the recording and then choose the correct answer.*

1）这____A____我的家。 　　A 是 　　B 不是

2）这是我爸爸妈妈的____B____。 　　A 卧室 　　B 房间

3）我家厨房在客厅的____B____。 　　A 后边 　　B 旁边

4）卫生间在卧室的____A____。 　　A 北边 　　B 对面

5）京京的房间很____A____。 　　A 漂亮 　　B 好看

Listen 3 *Listen to the recording and then tick the correct box.*

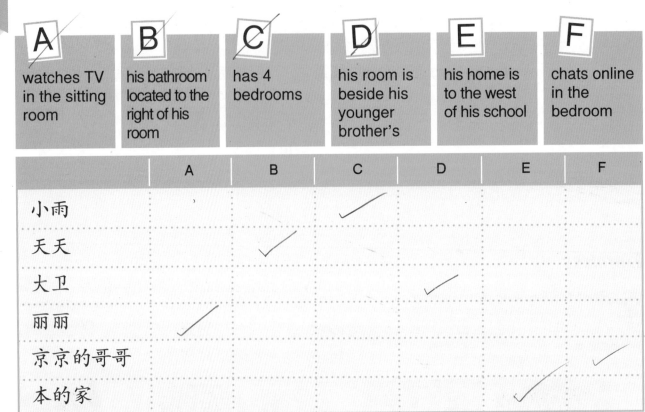

	A	B	C	D	E	F
	watches TV in the sitting room	his bathroom located to the right of his room	has 4 bedrooms	his room is beside his younger brother's	his home is to the west of his school	chats online in the bedroom
小雨			✓			
天天		✓				
大卫				✓		
丽丽	✓					
京京的哥哥						✓
本的家				✓		

Read 4 *Complete the sentences according to the pictures.*

① B 这是_____。
A 你的学校　B 我的家

② B 你家真_____。
A 不大　B 漂亮

③ B 客厅在_____。
A 北面　B 南面

④ A 卫生间在客厅_____。
A 旁边　B 对面

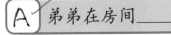
⑤ A 弟弟在房间_____。
 A 上网　 B 看书

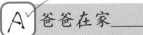
⑥ A 爸爸在家_____。
A 喝茶　B 看电视

Read 5 Read the following paragraph and answer the questions below in Chinese.

　　这个暑假我打算去伦敦旅行。我想住在我朋友大卫的家。去年，我去了他家，认识了他的爸爸妈妈。他家不大，有四个房间，每个房间都很漂亮。大卫的卧室在南边，他爸爸妈妈的卧室在北边。大卫家的客厅在西边，他的爸爸妈妈常常在客厅看电视，他们喜欢看新闻。大卫喜欢看比赛，我也喜欢看。

（比赛 上方标注：match）

Questions:

1) Where does the narrator want to stay?
In their friend David's house ✓

2) Which city is David's home in?
London ✓

3) When did the narrator go to David's home for the first time?
Last year ✓

4) How many rooms are there in David's house?
4 ✓

5) Where is David's bedroom?
South of the house ✓

6) Where is David's parents' bedroom?
north of the house ✓

7) Where is the living room? What do David's parents usually do in the living room?
west of the house, they often watch TV ✓

Talk 6 Talk about the pictures in Chinese.

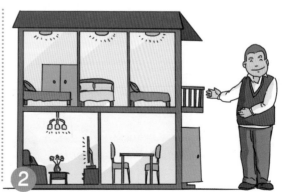

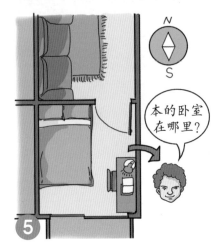

Write 7 *Complete the sentences with the proper Chinese characters.*

1）卫 生 间 (wèishēngjiān) 在我房间的对面。

2）你家真 漂 亮 (piàoliang)。

3）我的卧室在 东 (dōng) 边。

4）客厅在 南 (nán) 边吗？

5）西 (xī) 边的房间很大。

Talk 8 *Look at the picture and answer the following questions in Chinese.*

1）How many rooms are there in Zhou Ying's house? 八

2）Where is the living room? 北边

3）Where is Zhou Ying's parents' bedroom? 西北边

4）Where is Zhou Ying's bedroom? 东边

5）Where is the bathroom? 西南边

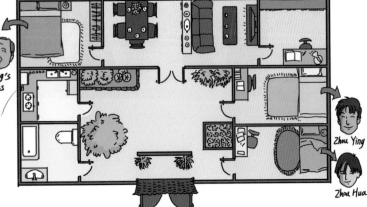

Write
9

Write the following Chinese characters.

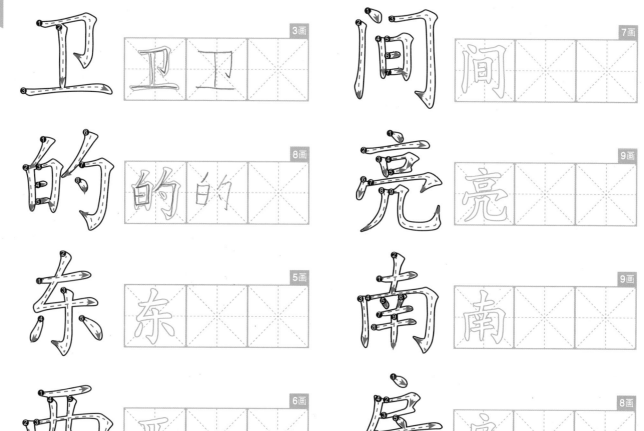

Read
10

Phonetics.

歌谣(A Rhyme)
Gēyáo

落叶
Luò yè

秋风秋风吹吹，
Qiūfēng qiūfēng chuī chuī,

树叶树叶飞飞，
shùyè shùyè fēi fēi,

就像一群蝴蝶，
jiù xiàng yì qún húdié,

张开翅膀追追。
zhāng kāi chìbǎng zhuī zhuī.

第五课 *Lesson* **5**

My Room Is Not Very Big 我的房间不大

Learning Objectives

交际话题 Topic of conversation:
处所位置 Location
Chùsuǒ wèizhì

基本句型 Sentence patterns:
我的房间在……边。
房间里有椅子、桌子。
客厅里有沙发。
书架上有很多中文书。

New Words

1. 里 lǐ **prep.** in, among
2. 床 chuáng **n.** bed
3. 桌子 zhuōzi **n.** table
4. 椅子 yǐzi **n.** chair
5. 沙发 shāfā **n.** sofa
6. 书架 shūjià **n.** bookshelf
7. 电脑 diànnǎo **n.** computer
8. 杂志 zázhì **n.** magazine
9. 干净 gānjìng **adj.** clean
10. 门 mén **n./m.w.** door; (a measure word used for school subjects)
11. 窗户 chuānghu **n.** window
12. 花园 huāyuán **n.** garden
13. 笔 bǐ **n.** pen

Text

Part I

京京：这是你的房间吗？

大海：不是，这是我哥哥的

　　　房间，我的房间在旁边。

京京：你的房间大吗？

大海：我的房间不大。

京京：你的房间里有什么？
　　　　　　　　lǐ

大海：我的房间里有床、桌子、
　　　　　　　　　　chuáng zhuōzi

　　　椅子、沙发和书架。
　　　yǐzi　　shāfā　　shūjià

京京：你的电脑在哪儿？
　　　　　diànnǎo

大海：电脑在桌子上。我常常用电脑

　　　上网。

京京：房间里有电视吗？

大海：没有，电视在客厅里。我常常

　　　在客厅里看电视。

京京：你喜欢什么电视节目？

大海：我喜欢看足球比赛。

京京：你喜欢看什么书？

大海：我喜欢看中文书。我的书架

　　　上有很多中文书和杂志。
　　　　　　　　　　　　zázhì

Part II

我的房间不大

这就是我的房间。房间不大，很干净。门的对面是窗户，窗户外边有
This exactly is my room.　My room isn't big,　gānjìng　mén　　chuānghu　outside the window
　　　　　　　　　　　very clean.　The door is opposite the
　　　　　　　　　　　　　　　　　window.

一个漂亮的花园。
huāyuán
is a beautiful garden.

我的桌子上有电脑、笔和书。我常常用电脑上网看新闻、发电子邮件
on my table there is a computer, bǐ *a pen and book. I often use the computer to go online and to send emails*
read the news

和聊天儿。明天上午有中文课，我现在要读中文书。我的爸爸、妈妈正在
and to chat. next week I have a chinese lesson, *my dad, mum*

客厅看电视，他们喜欢看新闻。客厅里有两个书架，书架上有很多书，也
watch TV in the living room, they like to watch the news. In the living room there are 2 bookshelves, on the bookshelf there are also lots of books.

有很多杂志。我们都喜欢看书。
lots of magazines. Our favorite is to read books.

Exercises

Read
1　*Read the following words and then match them with the proper pictures.*

A 桌子　　　　B 椅子　　　　C 沙发　　　　D 窗　　　　E 书架
F 杂志　　　　G 电脑　　　　H 笔　　　　　I 电视　　　　J 看新闻

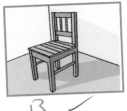    

....B....　　　....J....　　　....H....　　　....A....　　　....F....

....G....　　　....I....　　　....D....　　　....E....　　　....C....

Listen
2　*Listen to the recording and then choose the correct answer.*

1）你的____A____里有什么？　　　　　A 房间　　　　B 家

2）桌____B____上有一本书。　　　　　A 字　　　　　B 子

3）我用用你的____B____好吗？　　　　A 电视　　　　B 电脑

4）我喜欢这个红色的____B____。　　　A 书　　　　　B 笔

5）我朋友的家很____A____，也很漂亮。　A 干净　　　　B 好看

Listen
3 *Listen to the recording and then tick the correct box.*

	A					F
A there are many Chinese books	**B** there is a sofa and some chairs	**C** there is a small TV	**D** there is a computer	**E** there is a bookshelf		**F** likes to watch sports programmes

	A	B	C	D	E	F
我的卧室里						
我哥哥的卧室里						
客厅里						
爸爸						
姐姐的房间里						
桌子上						

Read
4 *Complete the sentences according to the pictures.*

1. 客厅里有__A__。

A 沙发　B 椅子

2. 大海在房间里_____。

A 玩电脑　B 看电视

3. 哥哥的房间真_____。

A 热　B 漂亮

4. 书架上有很多_____。

A 书和杂志　B 电话和电脑

5. 桌子上没有_____。

A 电脑　B 书

Read 5 *Read the following paragraph and answer the questions below in Chinese.*

　　这是小雨的房间，房间里有一个书架，书架上有很多书，也有很多杂志，有电影杂志，也有流行音乐杂志。小雨打算将来做演员，她知道 *plans future to be an actress* 很多有名的演员。她的房间里有一个电视，她常常看电视，她喜欢看音乐节目，也喜欢看电影。小雨的姐姐叫小美，她的房间在对面，房间里有电脑，没有电视，她常常上网。

Questions:

1) *What is on Xiaoyu's bookshelf?*

　　lots of books and magazines

2) *Which magazines does Xiaoyu have?*

　　movie magazines and pop music magazines

3) *What does Xiaoyu want to do when she grows up?*

　　be an actress

4) *Which television programmes does Xiaoyu like?*

　　music programmes

5) *Where is her elder sister's room?*

　　opposite

6) *What is there in her elder sister's room?*

　　computer but not TV

7) *What does her elder sister often do in her room?*

　　goes online

Talk 6 *Talk about the pictures in Chinese.*

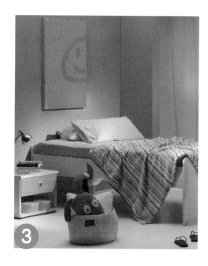

Write 7 *Complete the sentences with the proper Chinese characters.*

1）教室里有很多 (yǐzi)。

2）客厅里有 (shāfā)。

3）图书馆里有很多 (diànnǎo)。

4）你喜欢什么颜色 (yánsè, color) 的 (bǐ)?

5）你们的房间 (gānjìng) 吗?

Talk 8 *Answer the following questions in Chinese.*

1）What are there in the living room?

2）What are there in the study room?

3）What are there in Dahai's room?

4）What are there on Dahai's table?

5）What are there in the hotel room?

6）Is the hotel room big and clean?

Dahai's room

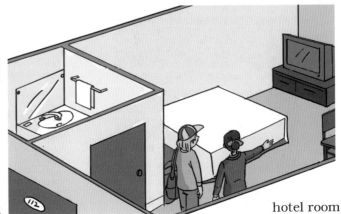
hotel room

Write 9 *Write the following Chinese characters.*

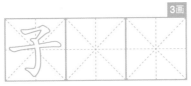
3画

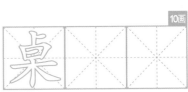
10画

7画

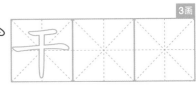
3画

10画

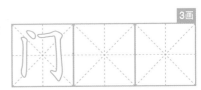
3画

Read 10 *Phonetics.*

歌谣(A Rhyme)
Gēyáo

我们的祖国是花园
Wǒmen de zǔguó shì huāyuán,

美丽的祖国是花园，　　花园的花朵真鲜艳。
Měilì de zǔguó shì huāyuán,　　huāyuán de huāduǒ zhēn xiānyàn.

和暖的阳光照耀着大地，　每个人脸上都笑开颜。
Hénuǎn de yángguāng zhàoyàozhe dàdì,　měi gè rén liǎn shàng dōu xiàokāi yán.

第六课 *Lesson*

My Home Is in the City Centre

我的家在市中心

6

Learning Objectives

交际话题 **Topic of conversation:**
处所位置 Location
Chùsuǒ wèizhi

基本句型 **Sentence patterns:**
我家在市中心。
从我家到学校不远。
电影院在我家左边。
广场很热闹。

New Words

1. 市中心 shì zhōngxīn **n.** city centre; downtown
2. 从 cóng **prep.** from
3. 到 dào **v.** to get to; to arrive
4. 远 yuǎn **adj.** far
5. 附近 fùjìn **adv.** nearby; in the vicinity of
6. 电影院 diànyǐngyuàn **n.** cinema
7. 有时候 yǒushíhou **adv.** sometimes
8. 购物 gòu wù **v.** to go shopping
9. 购物中心 gòuwù zhōngxīn **n.** shopping centre
10. 广场 guǎngchǎng **n.** square, plaza
11. 热闹 rènao **adj.** busy, bustling
12. 画画儿 huà huàr **v.** to draw; to paint a picture
13. 那里 nàli **pron.** there; over there

Text

Part I

天天：你家在哪儿？

大海：我家在市中心。
　　　　shì zhōngxīn

天天：从你家到学校远吗？
　　　cóng　dào　　yuǎn

大海：从我家到学校不远，我骑

　　　自行车去上学。

天天：你家附近有电影院吗？
　　　　　fùjìn　diànyǐngyuàn

大海：有一个电影院。你喜欢看

　　　电影吗？

天天：是的。你呢？

大海：我也喜欢。周末我有时候
　　　　　　　　　　yǒushíhou

　　　去看电影。我喜欢美国

　　　电影。

天天：你和谁一起看电影？

大海：我和朋友一起看电影。你常
　　　　　　　to go

　　　到市中心吗？

天天：我常和妈妈去市中心购物。
　　　　　　　　　　　　　gòu wù

大海：购物中心前边的广　场很
　　　gòuwù zhōngxīn　　　guǎngchǎng

　　　热闹，我也常常去那里。
　　　rènao　　　　　　　nàli

Part II

我家在市中心

我家在市中心，从我家到学校不远，我每天走路去学校。从星期一到星

I live in the city centre, it is not far from my house to school, everyday I walk to school. On monday to Friday

期五我都有课。周末我休息，我和爸爸常常去运动场做运动。我家附近有一
I have lessons. On weekends I have a rest, Me and my dad often go to a sports field to do sports. My home has one cinema

个电影院，爸爸有时候开车和我去看电影。购物中心在我家北边，周末我妈
nearby

妈和姐姐常常去购物。购物中心旁边的广场很热闹，有很多画家，他们在

那儿画画儿。周末广场上有音乐会，暑假的晚上我常常去那里听音乐。
huà huàr

Exercises

Read 1 *Read the following words and then match them with the proper pictures.*

A 远   **B** 画画儿   **C** 电影院   **D** 市中心
E 热闹   **F** 购物中心   **G** 图书馆   **H** 体育馆

Listen 2 *Listen to the recording and then choose the correct answer.*

1）你家在 ___A___ ？   A 哪儿   B 那里

2）我家在 ___B___ 。   A 购物中心   B 市中心

3）从你家到学校 ___A___ 吗？   A 远   B 冷

4）你怎么去电影 ___A___ ？   A 院   B 远

5）你家旁边的 ___A___ 大吗？   A 广场   B 运动

Listen
3 Listen to the recording and then tick the correct box.

A	B	C	D	E	F
is drawing in the square	is in the city centre	there is a concert	cycles to school every day	likes shopping	is going to see a film on the weekend

	A	B	C	D	E	F
天天家		✓				
大卫				✓		
京京						✓
小雨					✓	
画家	✓					
广场上			✓			

Read
4 Complete the sentences according to the pictures.

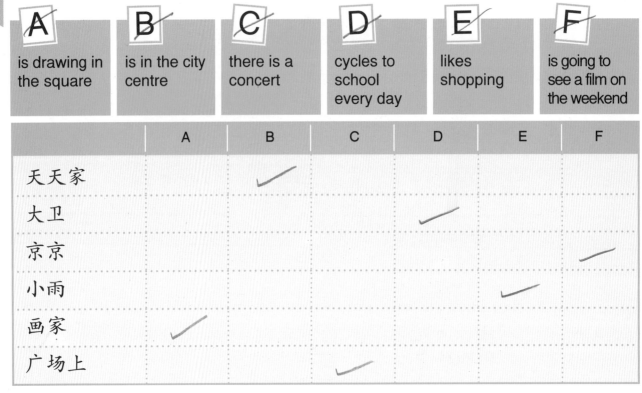

1. A　我家在＿＿＿。
   A 市中心　B 飞机场

2. B　我家旁边有个＿＿＿。
   A 体育馆　B 电影院

3. A　从你家到火车站＿＿＿吗?
   A 远　B 热闹

4. A　天天骑自行车去＿＿＿。
   A 图书馆　B 电影院

5. A　＿＿＿很热闹。
   A 广场　B 运动场

6. B　＿＿＿去上学。
   A 骑自行车　B 开车

Read **5** *Read the following paragraph and answer the questions below in Chinese.*

我的学校在市中心。学校旁边有一个小广场，广场附近有电影院、购物中心和图书馆。小广场很热闹，很多人去电影院看电影。今天有一个新电影，是中国电影，女演员很有名。大卫很喜欢看中国电影，今天下午我们没有课，我们一起去看这个新电影。电影院在我们学校的北边，从我们学校到电影院不远，我们骑自行车去。

Questions:

1) Where is the narrator's school located?

city center 市中心

2) What is there beside the school?

a small square 小广场

3) What is there on the square?

电影院 cinema, 购物中心 shopping center and 图书馆 library

4) What is on at the cinema today?

a chinese film 中国电影

5) What are they going to do this afternoon?

watch a film 看电影

6) How far is the cinema from the school?

it is not far 不远

7) How can they get there?

by bus 骑自行车去

Talk **6** *Talk about the pictures in Chinese.*

Write 7 *Complete the sentences with the proper Chinese characters.*

1）火车站在   （shì zhōngxīn）。

2）学校旁边有一个 物（gòu wù）中心。

3）电影 （yuàn）里有很多人。

4）（cóng）他家 到（dào）市中心不远。

5）今天这个 广 场（guǎngchǎng）真热闹！

Talk 8 *Answer the following questions in Chinese.*

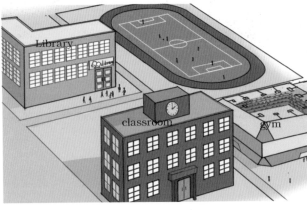 

1）Where is the library located?

2）Where is the gym located?

3）Where is the classroom building?

4）Where is the train station?

5）Where is the bus station?

6）Which place is the busiest?

Write 9 *Write the following Chinese characters.*

 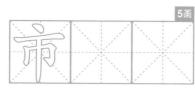

 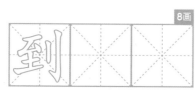

 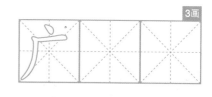

Read 10 *Phonetics.*

孔子语录(Confucius Quotes)
Kǒngzǐ yǔlù

论语 · 学而
Lúnyǔ · xué ér

春秋时期 · 孔子
Chūnqiū shíqī · Kǒng zǐ

学而时习之，不亦说乎？有朋自远方来，不亦乐乎？
Xué ér shí xí zhī, bú yì yuè hū? Yǒu péng zì yuǎnfāng lái, bú yì lè hū?

人不知而不愠，不亦君子乎？
Rén bù zhī ér bú yùn, bú yì jūnzǐ hū?

北京的四合院

　　四合院指东、西、南、北四面的房子围在一起，形成一个"口"字形的住宅结构。四合院在中国的民居中历史很悠久，距今约有三千多年；它的分布也很广泛，而北京胡同里的四合院更是驰名中外。正规四合院一般坐北朝南，四合院中的东、西、南、北四个方向的房子都可以居住。而北房作为正房，是院主人的住房。

Siheyuan, the Chinese Quadrangle

A *Siheyuan*, the Chinese quadrangle, is normally built in a structure like the Chinese character 口. The rooms on the east, west, south and north sides are arranged as a square. Among the residential buildings in China, *Siheyuan* has a long history of over 3,000 years and was commonly found, most famously in Beijing's *hutong*. The rooms that sit the north and face the south are considered the main ones. People can live in the rooms on all sides of the quadrangle.

第二单元小结　Unit Two　Summary

1 这/那+就是+宾语。 This/that + is + object.	这就是我的家。 This is my home. 那就是我们的图书馆。 That is our library.
2 名词+在+方位词。 Noun+ is + in + (a certain) direction.	卧室在东边。 The bedroom is in the east. 客厅在南边。 The living room is in the south. 卫生间在后边。 The bathroom is at the back.
3 某人的+名词+在+方位词。 Sb.'s + noun + is + on + (a certain) direction.	我的房间在旁边。 My room is on the side. 爸爸的书架在左边。 Dad's bookshelf is on the left.
4 名词+里+有+宾语。 Noun + inside + there be + object.	房间里有椅子和桌子。 There is a chair and a table in the room. 客厅里有沙发。 There is a sofa in the living room.
5 名词+上+有+宾语。 Noun + on + have + object.	书架上有很多中文书。 There are many Chinese books on the bookshelf. 桌子上有乒乓球。 There are table tennis balls on the table.
6 主语+在+某个方位。 Subject + is + in + (a certain) direction.	购物中心在我家右边。 The shopping centre is to the right of my home. 电影院在我家左边。 The cinema is on the left side of my home.
7 从+某处₁+到+某处₂＋（不/很)+远。 From + somewhere₁ + to + somewhere₂ + (not) + far.	从我家到学校不远。 The school is not far from our home. 从学校到电影院很远。 The cinema is far from the school.
8 某处+很+形容词。 Somewhere + very + adjective.	广场很热闹。 The square is very lively. 购物中心很大。 The shopping centre is very big.

第七课 **Lesson** **7**

What Do You Want to Buy? 你们想买什么？

Learning Objectives

交际话题 Topic of conversation:

超市购物
Chāoshì gòu wù
Shopping in the Supermarket

基本句型 Sentence patterns:
我什么都吃。我不买什么。
我买点心和苹果。
我还要牛奶。我请你们喝茶。

New Words

1　超市 chāoshì　**n.** supermarket
2　买 mǎi　**v.** to buy, to purchase
3　点心 diǎnxin　**n.** light refreshments; desserts
4　还 hái　**adv.** also, too; as well; in addition
5　一些/些 yìxiē/xiē　**adv.** some; a few
6　草莓 cǎoméi　**n.** strawberry
7　请 qǐng　**v.** to invite
8　来 lái　**v.** to come
9　东西 dōngxi　**n.** thing, object
10　鸡 jī　**n.** chicken
11　鸭 yā　**n.** duck
12　猪肉 zhūròu　**n.** pork
13　蛋糕 dàngāo　**n.** cake

Text

Part I

大卫：小雨、京京，你们去哪儿？

小雨：我们去超市。
chāoshì

大卫：你们要买什么？
mǎi

小雨：我买点心和牛奶，还想
diǎnxin　　　　hái
买一些草莓。
yìxiē　cǎoméi

大卫：京京，你呢？你买什么？

京京：我不买什么。

小雨：大卫，你也去超市吗？

大卫：不，我去电影院，我想看
电影。

京京：今天有什么电影？

大卫：有一个新电影，很好看。

京京：小雨，我们也去看电影，好吗？

小雨：好，我们先看电影，再去
超市买东西。

京京：好。电影院有一个喝茶的地
方，大卫，我请你们喝茶。
qǐng

大卫：我请你们吃点心。

Part II

我请朋友来我家

明天是我的生日，我请了很多朋友来我家。今天我和爸爸、妈妈要去
lái

超市，我们要买很多东西。这个超市很大，什么东西都有，妈妈想买鸡、
　　　　　　　　dōngxi　　　　　　　　　　　　　　　　　　　　　jī

鸭和牛肉，爸爸不喜欢牛肉，他想买鱼和猪肉。妈妈想买些蔬菜和水果，
yā　　　　　　　　　　　　　　　　　　　　zhūròu

爸爸还想买点心和果汁。我什么都喜欢吃，买什么我都高兴。我要买一个

蛋糕，我要请我的朋友吃生日蛋糕。
dàngāo

Exercises

Read 1 *Read the following words and then match them with the proper pictures.*

A 超市　　　　**B** 鸡和鸭　　　　**C** 点心和水果　　　**D** 喝牛奶
E 买东西　　　**F** 生日蛋糕　　　**G** 草莓和苹果　　　**H** 果汁和茶

　　F　　　　　　　G　　　　　　　B　　　　　　　C

  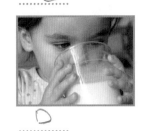

　　E　　　　　　　A　　　　　　　H　　　　　　　D

Listen 2 *Listen to the recording and then choose the correct answer.*

1）我和京京去____A____。　　　　　A 超市　　　　B 教师

2）爸爸想买____A____和水果。　　　A 海鲜　　　　B 点心

3）他们买了汽水，____A____有草莓。A 还　　　　　B 都

4）他请我们吃____A____。　　　　　A 蛋糕　　　　B 面包

5）妈妈去超市买____B____。　　　　A 鱼和牛肉　　B 鸡肉和鸭肉

Listen
3

Listen to the recording and then tick the correct box.

A	**B**	**C**	**D**	**E**	**F**
is not buying anything	invites us to her house	milk and desserts	likes to eat anything	is not going to the supermarket	chicken or duck

	A	B	C	D	E	F
京京					✓	
大海买了			✓			
小雨不吃						✓
大卫				✓		
丽丽请我们		✓				
玛丽不买	✓					

Read
4

Complete the sentences according to the pictures.

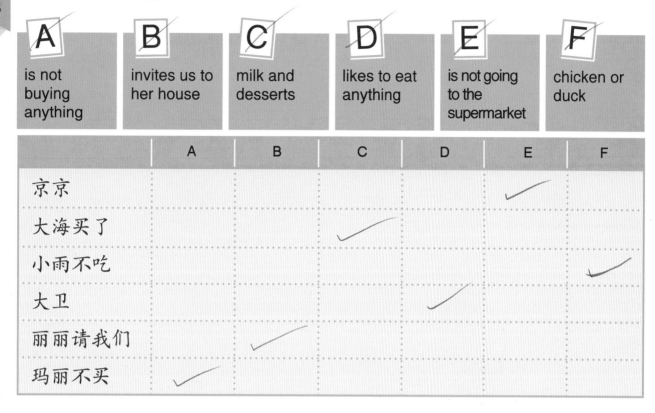

①  B 他们不去_____。

A 超市 **B** 电影院

②  A _____很大，也很红！

A 草莓 **B** 苹果

③  4 她_____我吃蛋糕。

A 请 **B** 想

④  B 他要牛奶，_____要点心。

A 不 **B** 还

⑤  A _____

A 他什么东西都买。 **B** 他不买什么东西。

Read
5
Read the following paragraph and answer the questions below in Chinese.

　　Josh的家在市中心，他家旁边有一个大超市，超市里什么东西都有。Josh每个周末都和妈妈去这个超市买东西，他们买很多东西，买鸡、鸭、牛肉、猪肉，还买蔬菜、水果、牛奶和果汁。这些（zhèxiē，these）东西Josh都喜欢，他还喜欢点心，今天他要买很多点心，还要买一个蛋糕，因为（yīnwèi，because）明天是他的生日，他要请朋友和同学来他家吃蛋糕。

Questions:

1) *Where does Josh live?*

....

2) *What is next to Josh's home?*

....

3) *What does Josh usually do on the weekends?*

....

4) *What do they buy?*

....

5) *Why does Josh want to buy a lot of light refreshments today?*

....

6) *What is Josh going to do tomorrow?*

....

Talk
6
Talk about your shopping experiences in Chinese according to the pictures.

Write 7 Complete the sentences with the proper Chinese characters.

1）我周末常常去 ☐☐ (chāoshì) 购物，我 ☐ (mǎi) 很多东西。

2）他买面包，他 ☐☐ (hái mǎi) 牛奶。

3）朋友 ☐ (qǐng) 我看电影，我 ☐ (qǐng) 他喝咖啡。

4）这个超市很大，有很多 ☐☐ (dōngxi)。

5）我不吃 ☐ (jī)、☐ (yā)，也不吃牛肉、猪肉。

Talk 8 Answer the following questions in Chinese.

1）Where do they go after school?
2）Does Mark want to buy anything?
3）What does Julie want to buy?
4）What about Ann?
5）What do you usually buy in a supermarket?

Julie   Ann   Mark

Write 9 *Write the following Chinese characters.*

 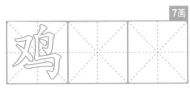

 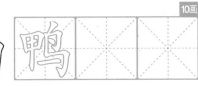

Read 10 *Phonetics.*

歌谣(A Rhyme)
Gēyáo

网上购物
Wǎng shàng gòu wù

在家购物鼠标点，
Zài jiā gòu wù shǔbiāo diǎn,

省时省力又省钱。
shěng shí shěng lì yòu shěng qián.

足不出户等收货，
Zú bù chū hù děng shōu huò,

网上购物真方便。
wǎng shàng gòu wù zhēn fāngbiàn.

第九课 *Lesson* **8**

How Much Is It Altogether? 一共多少钱?

Learning Objectives

交际话题 Topic of conversation:
了解价格 Talking About Prices
Liǎojiě jiàgé

基本句型 Sentence patterns:
苹果多少钱一斤?
草莓太贵了。我要一斤半。
三十块钱一个。

New Words

1 新鲜 xīnxiān **adj.** fresh

2 钱 qián **n.** money

3 斤 jīn **n.** *jin* (a unit in the Chinese weight system)

4 元/块 yuán/kuài **n.** yuan/*kuai* (a unit of Chinese money)

5 角/毛 jiǎo/máo **n.** *jiao/mao* (a unit of Chinese money

6 太 tài **adv.** too, extremely

7 贵 guì **adj.** expensive

8 一共 yígòng **adv.** altogether; in all

9 英镑/镑 yīngbàng/bàng **n.** pound, sterling

10 人民币 rénmínbì **n.** reminbi (the currency of China)

11 这里 zhèli **pron.** here

12 瓶 píng **m.w.** (a measure word used for bottles, jars)

13 便宜 piányi **adj.** cheap

Text

| Part I |

张先生：你想买什么？

大　海：我想买一些水果。

张先生：今天的苹果和草莓都很新鲜。
　　　　　　　　　　　　　　　xīnxiān

大　海：苹果多少钱一斤？
　　　　　　　　qián　jīn

张先生：四块五毛一斤，很便宜。
　　　　　　　máo　　　piányi

大　海：四块五毛，我要两斤。

张先生：好。还要草莓吗？

大　海：草莓多少钱？

张先生：草莓十二块一斤。
　　　　　　　　　kuài

大　海：草莓太贵了。
　　　　　　tài guì

张先生：不贵，超市的草莓二十块
　　　　　一斤。

大　海：好吧，我要一斤半。

　　　　　一共多少钱？
　　　　　yígòng

张先生：一共二十七块。

| Part II |

超市的东西不太贵

　　我是英国人，现在我在北京读中学。我很喜欢我的学校，也喜欢北京的家。我家旁边有一个购物中心，还有一个大超市。周末我常常去超市买东西。在英国买东西，我用英镑。在中国买东西，不用英镑，用人民币。
yīngbàng   rénmínbì

今天去超市，我要买牛奶、面包和水果。这里的东西不太贵，牛奶三
                                              zhèlì

元一瓶，面包两元一个，苹果、草莓也很新鲜。今天的蛋糕很便宜，小蛋
    píng

糕二十块钱一个，大蛋糕五十块钱一个。

Exercises

Read
1 Read the following words and then match them with the proper pictures.

A 英镑   B 太贵了   C 两瓶水   D 四斤半
E 三块九毛   F 没有什么钱   G 人民币   H 青菜便宜

....

....

Listen
2 Listen to the recording and then choose the correct answer.

1) 苹果多少钱_____?   A 一瓶   B 一斤

2) 点心_____一斤。   A 八块九   B 八毛九

3) 草莓太_____了。   A 便宜   B 贵

4) 请问，_____多少钱?   A 一共   B 一起

5) 他们都用_____。   A 英镑   B 英语

6) 鸡和鸭一共_____。   A 七斤八   B 七斤半

Listen 3 *Listen to the recording and then tick the correct box.*

	A	B	C	D	E	F
A spends 26.30 yuan	**B** wants to buy three apples	**C** buys strawberries	**D** wants to buy six bottles of water	**E** has some renminbi	**F** is not expensive	

	A	B	C	D	E	F
京京						
大海						
小雨						
大卫的生日蛋糕						
丽丽						
玛丽						

Read 4 *Complete the sentences according to the pictures.*

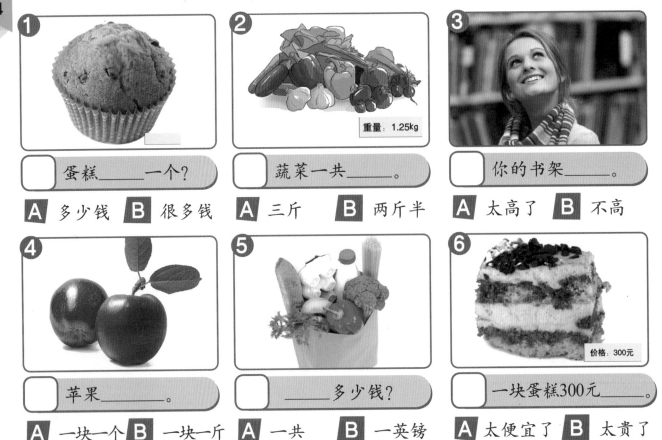

① 蛋糕_____一个？
　A 多少钱　B 很多钱

② 重量：1.25kg
　蔬菜一共_____。
　A 三斤　　B 两斤半

③ 你的书架_____。
　A 太高了　B 不高

④ 苹果_____。
　A 一块一个　B 一块一斤

⑤ _____多少钱？
　A 一共　　B 一英镑

⑥ 价格：300元
　一块蛋糕300元_____。
　A 太便宜了　B 太贵了

Read 5

Read the following paragraph and answer the questions below in Chinese.

　　市中心有一个大超市，这里什么东西都有。我家旁边有一个小超市，小超市里的东西不太多。大超市的东西很便宜，苹果一块八一斤，草莓十二块一斤，牛奶三块一瓶。小超市的东西比大超市贵，苹果两块一斤，草莓十三块九一斤，牛奶三块五一瓶。大超市还卖（mài, to sell）桌子、椅子和书，小超市没有。

Questions:

1) *Where are the two supermarkets?*

....

2) *Which supermarket has got everything?*

....

3) *Which supermarket has got cheaper goods?*

....

4) *What are the prices for apples, strawberries and milk in these two supermarkets?*

....

5) *What kinds of product can't you find in the small supermarket?*

....

Talk 6

Talk about the goods in the shopping centre and their prices in Chinese according to the pictures.

Write
7

Complete the sentences with the proper Chinese characters.

1）苹果 ☐ ☐ ☐ (duōshao qián) 一斤？

2）30块钱一个苹果，☐ ☐ (tài guì)了。

3）这个超市的东西很 ☐ ☐ (piányi)，很多人去买。

4）这本中文书9英镑，那本英文杂志8英镑，☐ ☐ (yígòng)

17英镑。

5）☐ ☐ (yì píng) 牛奶3元，☐ ☐ (yì jīn) 草莓15元。

Talk
8

Answer the following questions in Chinese.

28.9元　15.8元　106.00元

137.50元　无　无

supermaket

20.00/本　无

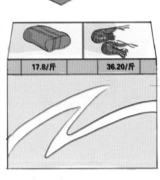

17.8/斤　36.20/斤

143.50/个　106.00/个

1）What can you buy on the Internet? What are the prices of things?

2）What can't you buy in this online shop?

3）What can you get in a supermarket? What are the prices of things?

4）Where do you often go shopping?

5）Where do you prefer to shop, online or at a supermarket?

Write
9

Write the following Chinese characters.

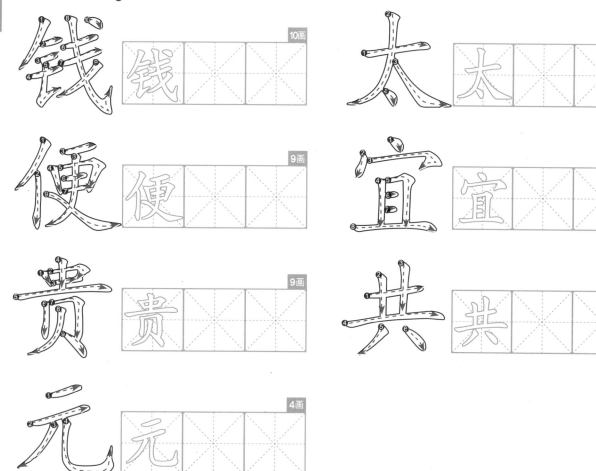

Read
10

Phonetics.

绕口令(A Rhyme)
Ràokǒulìng

小花鼓
Xiǎo huā gǔ

墙上一个鼓，　鼓上画老虎。
Qiáng shàng yì gè gǔ,　gǔ shàng huà lǎohǔ.

老虎扯破鼓，　拿块布来补。
Lǎohǔ chě pò gǔ,　ná kuài bù lái bǔ.

到底布补鼓，　还是布补虎？
Dàodǐ bù bǔ gǔ,　háishi bù bǔ hǔ?

第九课 **Lesson** **9**

I've Caught a Cold 我感冒了

Learning Objectives

交际话题 Topic of conversation:
生病与请假
Shēng bìng yǔ qǐng jià
Being Sick and Asking for Day(s) Off

基本句型 Sentence patterns:
他感冒了。
我头疼、咳嗽。
我跟你一样，也感冒了。
我今天不能去学校，我要请假。

New Words

1. 头 tóu **n.** head
2. 疼 téng **adj.** aching, painful
3. 咳嗽 késou **v.** to cough
4. 感冒 gǎnmào **n./v.** cold; to catch a cold
5. 跟 gēn **prep.** with, as
6. 一样 yíyàng **adj.** the same
7. 医院 yīyuàn **n.** hospital
8. 能 néng **v.** can; to be able to
9. 请假 qǐng jià to ask for day(s) off
10. 帮/帮助 bāng/bāngzhù **v.** to help
11. 回 huí **v.** to return
12. 生病 shéng bìng **v.** to fall ill

Text

Part I

小雨： 大海，早上好。我是小雨。

你在学校吗？

大海： 我不在学校，我在家。

小雨： 你在家？你怎么了？

大海： 我头疼、咳嗽。妈妈说，我
　　　tóu téng　 késou

感冒了。
gǎnmào

小雨： 我跟你一样，也感冒了。
　　　gēn　　yíyàng

大海： 你去医院了吗？
　　　　　yīyuàn

小雨： 我现在在医院。

大海： 医生说什么？

小雨： 医生说，我今天不能去学校。
　　　　　　　　　　　 néng

你能帮我请假吗？
　　bāng　 qǐng jià

大海： 能。我也要请假，我正在

给老师写电子邮件。

Part II

弟弟感冒了

星期日下午我和弟弟小海骑自行车去市中心的运动场，我们去看足
At sunday afternoon, my brother and I ride bicycle to the sports ground in the

球比赛了。从我家到运动场很远。天气太冷了，风很大，还下雨。晚上
city center to watch a football match. From the house to the sports ground is far. It is cold, windy

回家弟弟说他头疼，还咳嗽，他感冒了。他什么都不吃，什么都不喝。
huí jiā and raining In the evening, we return home and my brother says he has a headache, cough

今天我休息，不工作，我和弟弟去了医院。医生说，弟弟不能上学，要
and cold. He cannot eat or drink anything. Today, I rest and not work and I go

在家休息。弟弟给老师写了电子邮件：
with my brother to hospital. The doctor says that he can't go to school, need

to rest at home. My brother sends an email to the teacher, saying:

老师：

　　您好！

　　今天我生病了，头疼、咳嗽，不能去学校了，我想请假一天。"
　　　　shēng bìng

" Teacher: 小海

Hello!

I am sick today, headaches, coughing and cannot go to school.　6月3号

I want to take a day off please "　小海

Exercises

Read 1 *Match the English with the Chinese.*

A 头疼　　　B 不一样　　　C 想回家　　　D 去医院　　　E 感冒了

F 我跟你一样　　G 不能上课　　H 帮我请假　　I 能去学校吗　　J 咳嗽了

to go to the hospital	Can I go to school?	to have a cough
D	I	J

to have a cold	to want to go home	the same as you	headache
E	C	F	A

different	to ask for day off for me	to be unable to go to class
B	H	G

Listen 2 *Listen to the recording and then choose the correct answer.*

1) 我_____，我不想看书。　　　　　A 热闹　　B 头疼

2) 这个超市____那个超市一样，都很干净。　A 跟　　B 和

3) 他今天不_____去学校。　　　　　A 能　　B 想

4) 天气不好，很多人_____了。　　　　A 高兴　　B 感冒

5) 我跟你_____，也在医院。　　　　　A 一共　　B 一样

6) 他在_____，他要一些喝水。　　　　A 咳嗽　　B 请假

Listen 3 *Listen to the recording and then tick the correct box.*

A	B	C	D	E	F
has no headache, but has a cough	goes to hospital	is as ill as I am	doesn't want to go to the hospital	wants to ask for days off	has a headache and a cough

	A	B	C	D	E	F
天天						
大海						
小雨						
大卫						
丽丽						
玛丽						

Read 4 *Complete the sentences according to the pictures.*

1.
A 他＿＿＿＿，不想去看电影。
A 头疼　B 很冷

2.
B 这个蛋糕＿＿那个蛋糕＿＿。
A 和……一起　B 跟……一样

3.
B 她＿＿＿＿，不能表演。
A 唱歌　B 咳嗽

4.
B 我的书架跟他的书架＿＿＿＿。
A 一样　B 不一样

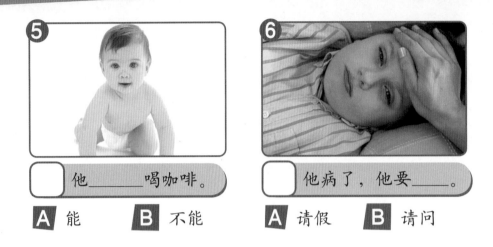

⑤ 他＿＿＿＿喝咖啡。

A 能 **B** 不能

⑥ 他病了，他要＿＿＿＿。

A 请假 **B** 请问

Read 5 *Read the following paragraph and answer the questions below in Chinese.*

今天是星期五，早上小海头很疼，还咳嗽。他妈妈跟他一起去医院，医生说："你叫小海吧？你感冒了，今天不能去学校上课，在家休息吧。"小海很高兴，他说："太好了，我要请假，我不去上课了。"医生说："你病了，你为什么（wèishénme, why）很高兴？"小海说："因为（yīnwèi, because）今天有数学课，我最不喜欢数学课。"

Questions:

1) How did Xiaohai feel in the morning?

..........he had a very bad headache..........

2) Where did he go with his mother?

..........to the hospital..........

3) What did the doctor say?

..........is xiaohai your name? You have a cold, in the morning you cannot go
4) What did Xiaohai say then? to school

....

5) Why was Xiaohai so pleased to be ill?

....

6) Would you be pleased to be ill?

....

Talk 6 Talk about the people in the hospital according to the pictures.

Write 7 Complete the sentences with the proper Chinese characters.

1）我 头 疼 (tóu téng)，什么都不想看。

2）这瓶水 跟 (gēn) 那瓶水 一 样 (yíyàng)，都很贵。

3）他是医生，他在 医 院 (yīyuàn) 工作。

4）她 咳 嗽 (késou) 了，她要请假。

5）大卫咳嗽两天了，他 能 (néng) 踢足球吗？

Talk 8 Answer the following questions in Chinese.

六十七 **67**

1） *What are the boys doing?*

2） *What's wrong with Dahai?*

3） *What's wrong with Ben?*

4） *What do their mothers say?*

Write 9 Write the following Chinese characters.

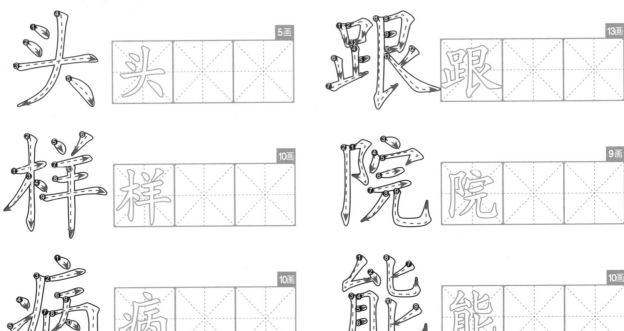

Read 10 *Phonetics.*

谚语(A Proverb)
Yànyǔ

一天一苹果，医生远离我。
Yì tiān yì píngguǒ,　yīshēng yuǎnlí wǒ.

一天三杯茶，不用把药拿。
Yì tiān sān bēi chá,　bú yòng bǎ yào ná.

文化常识 *Cultural Tip*

太极拳

太极拳起源于中国，是一项传统的武术、健身项目。这项运动历史悠久，流派众多，传播非常广泛。太极拳是武术、艺术、气功等的完美结合，练习时要讲究意、气、形的配合。

Tai Chi Chuan

Tai chi chuan, originated in China, is a traditional Chinese martial art practised for both defence training and health benefits. It has a very long history and a multitude of styles, and has spread all over the world. *Tai chi chuan* is a harmonious blend of kung fu, art and qigong. Practising *tai chi chuan* requires paying particular attention to combining a relaxed frame of mind, regulated natural breathing and smooth circular movements.

第三单元小结　Unit Three　Summary

1 某人+不+动词+什么。 Sb. + do not + verb + anything.	我不买什么。 I don't need to buy anything. 他不要什么。 He doesn't need anything.
2 某人+什么+都+动词。 Sb. + everything + all + verb.	我什么都吃。 I can eat everything. 他什么都喜欢。 He likes everything.
3 某人+还+要+食品/饮品。 Sb. + as well + want + food/drink.	我还要牛奶。 I want milk as well. 弟弟还要点心。 The younger brother wants snacks as well.
4 某人₁+请+某人₂+动词+宾语。 Sb.₁ + invite + sb.₂ + verb + object.	我请你们喝茶。 I'd like to invite you over for tea. 哥哥请朋友来我家。 My elder brother has invited a friend to our home.
5 某物+多少钱+数词+量词？ Sth. + how much + numeral + measure word?	苹果多少钱一斤？ How much is a *jin* of apples? 面包多少钱一个？ How much for a loaf of bread?
6 太+形容词+了。 Too + adjective + auxiliary word 了.	太便宜了。 Too cheap. 太大了。 Too big.
7 数词+块钱+数词+量词。 Numeral + measure word (for money) + numeral + measure word.	三十块钱一个。 30 yuan each. 五块钱一本。 Five yuan per book.
8 某人+要+数词+量词。 Sb. + want + numeral + measure word.	我要一斤。 I want one and a half jin. 爸爸要三个。 Dad wants three of then.

9 某人＋要＋动词(＋宾语)。 Sb. + want to + verb (+ object).	我要请假。 I want to take a day off. 妹妹要吃苹果。 The younger sister wants to eat an apple.
10 某人＋动词＋了。 Sb. + verb + auxiliary word 了.	他感冒了。 He has a cold. 历史老师请假了。 The history teacher took a day off.
11 某人＋某病症。 Sb. + a certain symptom.	我头疼、咳嗽。 I have a headache and a cough. 弟弟肚子 (dùzi) 疼。 The younger brother has a stomachache.
12 某人₁＋跟＋某人₂＋一样，也＋动词＋了。 Sb₁ + and + sb₂ + the same, also + verb + auxiliary word 了.	我跟你一样，也感冒了。 Just like you, I also have a cold. 他跟我一样，也请假了。 Just like me, he also has a cough.
13 某人＋时间名词＋（不）＋能＋动词＋宾语。 Sb. + time + (not) + can + verb + object.	我今天不能去学校。 I can't go to school today. 小雨明天能上课。 Xiaoyu can go to school tomorrow.

第十课 Lesson

10

我明天有汉语课
I Have a Chinese Lesson Tomorrow

Learning Objectives

交际话题 Topic of conversation:

学校学习 The School Day
Xuéxiào xuéxí

基本句型 Sentence patterns:

你今天上了什么课? 我今天上了体育课。

你明天有什么课? 我明天有汉语课。

New Words

1 体育 tǐyù **n.** physical education
2 数学 shùxué **n.** mathematics
3 历史 lìshǐ **n.** history
4 地理 dìlǐ **n.** geography
5 学期 xuéqī **n.** school term
6 德语 Déyǔ **n.** German
7 新 xīn **adj.** new
8 开始 kāishǐ **v.** to begin, to start
9 科学 kēxué **n.** science
10 有趣 yǒuqù **adj.** fun, interesting
11 时间表 shíjiānbiǎo **n.** timetable, schedule
12 放学 fàng xué classes are over

Text

Part I

（丽丽和天天在学校体育场旁边）

天天：丽丽，你今天上了什么课？

丽丽：我今天上了体育课，还上了
　　　tǐyù
　　　数学课和历史课。你呢？
　　　shùxué　　lìshǐ

天天：我也上了数学课，还上了音
　　　乐课和地理课。
　　　　　　dìlǐ

丽丽：这个学期你上什么外语课？
　　　　　xuéqī

天天：我上德语课，我喜欢德语。
　　　　　Déyǔ
　　　你呢？

丽丽：我上汉语课。这个学期的汉

语课很有趣。
　　yǒuqù

天天：你喜欢汉语课，太好了！

我帮你学汉语。你明天有

什么课？

丽丽：我明天有汉语课，还有

科学课。
kēxué

Part II

新学期开始了
　　　　　kāishǐ

　　新学期开始了。这学期跟上学期不一样，我有很多课。老师发了这

个学期的时间表，我们从星期一到星期五，每天上午上课，下午也上课，
　　　　shíjiānbiǎo

放学很晚，星期六和星期日休息。今天上午我上了英语课、数学课和音乐
fàng xué

课，下午上了地理课和体育课。这学期我们有一门新课——汉语课。我们

mén xīn

的汉语老师是中国人，她很漂亮，个子很高。我们班有25个学生，都喜欢上

汉语课。

Exercises

Read 1 Read the following words and then match them with the proper pictures.

A 历史课　　**B** 数学书　　**C** 地理书　　**D** 上科学课　　**E** 时间表

F 有趣　　**G** 德语　　**H** 上体育课

....　.............　.............　.............

....　.............　.............　.............

Listen 2 Listen to the recording and then choose the correct answer.

1）我今天上了_____。　　　A 数学课　　B 科学课

2）他是这个学校的_____老师。　A 历史　　　B 地理

3）我们这个_____有汉语课。　　A 学期　　　B 星期

4）今天的_____很有意思。　　　A 外语课　　B 汉语课

5）你有这个学期的_____吗?　　A 数学书　　B 时间表

Listen 3 Listen to the recording and then tick the correct box.

	A	B	C	D	E	F
A will have a science lesson tomorrow	**B** likes Chinese and Maths the most	**C** has no lessons	**D** has a timetable on the bookshelf	**E** has a foreign language lesson	**F** this term starts tomorrow	

	A	B	C	D	E	F
京京						
大海						
丽丽						
大卫						
小雨						
玛丽						

Read 4 Complete the sentences according to the pictures.

① 我五点____回家?

A 上学　　**B** 放学

② 今天我们上____课。

A 德语课　　**B** 乒乓球

③ 明天我们班有____。

A 英语课　　**B** 地理课

④ 这个学期的课程很____。

A 有趣　　**B** 没趣

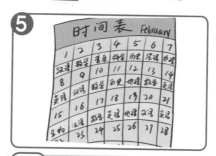

⑤ 这是____的时间表。

A 二月　　**B** 十二月

Read 5 *Read the following paragraph and answer the questions below in Chinese.*

今天是9月1日，新学期开始了。现在我是四年级 (niánjí, grade)，哥哥是六年级。我看了这个学期的时间表，我们的时间表不一样，哥哥的课比我的多，放学比我晚。我今天上了数学课、音乐课，还上了体育课。哥哥上了英语课、科学课和地理课。这个学期，我和哥哥都上汉语课，我星期一有汉语课，哥哥星期五有汉语课，我们的汉语老师都是李 (Lǐ, a surname) 老师。

Questions:

1) *When does the new term start?*

....

2) *Which grade are they in?*

....

3) *What has the narrator found that is different this term?*

....

4) *Which lessons does the narrator have today?*

....

5) *Which lessons does the narrator's brother have today?*

....

6) *What does the narrator and his brother have in common?*

....

Talk 6 *Talk about Ben's timetable today in Chinese according to the pictures.*

7:30	8:00—8:45	8:55—9:40	10:00—10:45
	English	Mathematics	Geography

10:55—11:40	Rest	13:30—14:15	14:25—15:10	15:30
Science		Chinese		

Complete the sentences with the proper Chinese characters.

1）我们的 ☐ ☐ (tǐyù) 老师是德国人。

2）我今天上了 ☐ ☐ ☐ (shùxuékè)。

3）我买了一本 ☐ ☐ ☐ (dìlǐshū) 和两本 ☐ ☐

☐ (lìshǐshū)。

4）他的爱好是运动，最喜欢上 ☐ ☐ (tǐyù) 课。

5）今天是9月1日，☐ (xīn) 学期开始了。

Answer the following questions in Chinese.

1）What is that on the table?
2）Which day is it today? What lesson did Mark have this morning?
3）What lesson did Mark have this afternoon? What did he do afterwards?
4）Which lessons will Mark have tomorrow?
5）Can you talk about your timetable?

星期三，上午   星期三，下午

Write 9 *Write the following Chinese characters.*

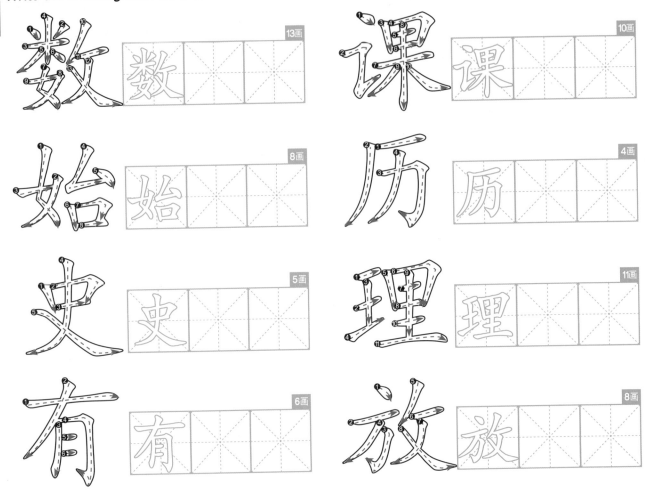

Read 10 *Phonetics.*

歌谣(A Rhyme)
Gē yáo

数星星
Shǔ xīngxing

弟弟抬头数星星， 数来数去数不清。
Dìdi tái tóu shǔ xīng xing， shǔlái–shǔqù shǔ bu qīng.

数不清， 数不清， 急得弟弟眨眼睛。
Shǔ bu qīng， shǔ bu qīng， jí de dìdi zhǎ yǎnjing.

第十一课 *Lesson* **11**

Is Chinese Difficult or Not? 汉语难不难？

Learning Objectives

交际话题 Topic of conversation:

谈论课程
Tánlùn kèchéng
Talking About Courses

基本句型 Sentence patterns:

汉语难不难？ 汉语不难。
什么课程最有趣？
我最喜欢历史。

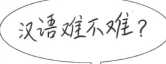

New Words

1 难 nán **adj.** difficult, hard

2 课程 kèchéng **n.** course, curriculum

3 作业 zuòyè **n.** homework

4 考试 kǎoshì **n.** examination, test

5 因为 yīnwèi **conj.** because

6 所以 suǒyǐ **conj.** therefore; as a result

7 成绩 chéngjì **n.** results, marks, achievements

8 容易 róngyì **adj.** easy

9 汉字 Hànzì **n.** Chinese character

10 昨天 zuótiān **n.** yesterday

11 科目 kēmù **n.** school subject

Text

Part I

大卫：丽丽，今天在学校里怎么样？

丽丽：很好。

大卫：你今天上了什么课？

丽丽：我今天上了英语课、数学课、音乐课和汉语课。

大卫：汉语难不难？
　　　nán

丽丽：汉语不难，我喜欢上汉语课。

大卫：你还喜欢什么课？

丽丽：我还喜欢地理课和历史课。

大卫：什么课程最有趣？
　　　　kèchéng

丽丽：历史课最有趣，我最喜欢历史。

大卫：你不喜欢数学课吗？

丽丽：不喜欢，数学太难了。

大卫：今天的作业多不多？
　　　　　zuòyè

丽丽：明天有考试，今天没有作业。
　　　　　kǎoshì

Part II

弟弟最喜欢的科目
kēmù

我弟弟是中学生，他学习的课程很多，他上英语课、数学课、科学课、历史课、地理课，还有音乐和体育。因为他喜欢运动，所以他喜欢体
yīnwèi　　　　　　　　suǒyǐ

育课，他的体育成绩也很好。今年他也开始学习汉语。他星期三和星期五

有汉语课，星期三他学习说汉语，星期五他学习写汉字。弟弟写的汉字很

Hànzì

漂亮，昨天他用汉语给老师写信，他说汉字很容易写。他的汉语老师是中

zuótiān　　　　　　　　　　　　　　　　　　　　　róngyì

国人，他很喜欢他的老师。现在他最喜欢的科目是汉语。他打算将来去中

国做一个记者，做电视新闻。

Exercises

Read 1 *Read the following words and expressions and then match them with the proper pictures.*

A 难　　　B 做作业　　　C 考试　　　D 汉字　　　E 课程表
F 老师帮学生　　　H 他的成绩好　　　I 用电话说

....

....

Listen 2 *Listen to the recording and then choose the correct answer.*

1) 今天有数学课和＿＿＿＿＿＿。　　　　A 音乐课　　　B 英语课

2) 我们的历史＿＿＿＿＿不难。　　　　　A 作业　　　　B 考试

3) 他姐姐在这个学校＿＿＿＿＿。　　　　A 教书　　　　B 学习

4) 最有意思的＿＿＿＿＿是科学。　　　　A 课程　　　　B 科目

5) 他们都喜欢＿＿＿＿＿汉语。　　　　　A 写　　　　　B 说

Listen
3

Listen to the recording and then tick the correct box.

A	B	C	D	E	F
has no homework today	likes the Chinese best	thinks history is interesting	writes Chinese characters every day	has a lot of homework	will have an exam tomorrow

	A	B	C	D	E	F
京京						
大海						
小雨						
大卫						
丽丽						
玛丽						

Read
4

Complete the sentences according to the pictures.

1

A _____最有意思。
A 科学课　B 体育课

2

B 历史课_____。
A 考试很难　B 作业很多

3

A 考试太_____了，我们都不会做。
A 难　　B 容易

A 什么课程最有意思?
B 我最喜欢这个课程。

4

A 他最喜欢_____。
A 写汉字　B 说汉语

5

A _____

Read 5 *Read the following paragraph and answer the questions below in Chinese.*

　　Josh今年十四岁，他在Wellington学校学习。他很喜欢学校的课程，学校的课程都很有意思，他最喜欢的科目是外语课。他现在学习汉语，他觉得 (juéde, to think, to feel) 汉语不太难。他每天说汉语，每天写汉字。昨天他用中文给我写信，他写得很好，他的汉字很漂亮。

Questions:

1) How old is Josh?

....

2) Where is he studying?

....

3) Does he like his courses at school?

....

4) Which subject does he like best?

....

5) Which foreign language is he studying now? What does he think about it?

....

6) What did he do yesterday? What did he think about it?

....

Talk 6 *Talk about Ben's Wednesday in Chinese according to the pictures.*

Write 7　Complete the sentences with the proper Chinese characters.

1）学校的 ☐ ☐ (kèchéng) 都很有意思。

2）今天的数学 ☐ ☐ (kǎoshì) 太 ☐ (nán) 了。

3）今天没有 ☐ ☐ (zuòyè)， 我去看电影。

4）☐ ☐ (yīnwèi) 写汉字太难了，☐ ☐ (suǒyǐ)

他不喜欢学汉语。

5）他说汉字很 ☐ ☐ (róngyì) 写。

Talk 8　Answer the following questions in Chinese.

1）Which courses does Ben like? Why?

2）Which courses doesn't he like? Why?

3）Which courses are you studying now?

4）Which subject do you like best? Why?

5）Which subject do you like least? Why?

Write 9 *Write the following Chinese characters.*

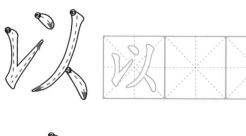 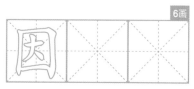

   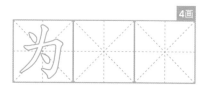

 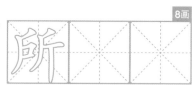  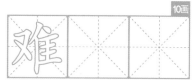

Read 10 *Phonetics.*

孔子语录(Confucius Quotes)
Kǒngzǐ yǔlù

论语 · 为 政
Lúnyǔ · wéi zhèng

春秋时期 · 孔子
Chūnqiū shíqī · Kǒngzǐ

知之为知之， 不知为不知， 是知也。
Zhī zhī wéi zhī zhī, bù zhī wéi bù zhī, shì zhī yě.

第十二课 *Lesson* **12**

Let's Play Ping-pong! 来打乒乓球吧!

Learning Objectives

交际话题 Topic of conversation:

课外活动 Extracurricular
Kèwài huódòng Activities

基本句型 Sentence patterns:

你太胖了。
来打乒乓球吧!
我们去打羽毛球。
你们踢不踢足球?

New Words

1 来 lái **v.** (used before a verb to express an intention to do sth.)

2 羽毛球 yǔmáoqiú **n.** badminton

3 少 shǎo **adj./adv.** few, less; seldom, hardly ever

4 胖 pàng **adj.** fat, obese

5 棒球 bàngqiú **n.** baseball

6 踢 tī **v.** to kick, to play (football)

7 觉得 juéde **v.** to think, to feel

8 健康 jiànkāng **n./adj.** health; healthy, vigorous

9 溜冰 liū bīng **v./n.** to skate; ice skating

10 办法 bànfǎ **n.** way to handle affairs; method

11 走路 zǒu lù **v.** to walk; to go on foot

Text

Part I

大海：弟弟，来打乒乓球吧！
　　　　　 lái

　　　你看，你的朋友也在打。

弟弟：我不打，我不会打乒乓球。

大海：你会打羽毛球，我们去打羽毛球。
　　　　　　　 yǔmáoqiú

弟弟：我也不想打，我想吃蛋糕。

大海：你不能再吃蛋糕了！

弟弟：那我能吃什么？

大海：什么都不能吃。你要少吃东西，
　　　　　　　　　　　 shǎo

　　　多运动，你太胖了。
　　　　　　　　 pàng

弟弟：我不喜欢运动，太没意思了。

大海：你喜欢打棒球吗？打棒球很有
　　　　　　　 bàngqiú

　　　意思。

弟弟：不，我不喜欢。

大海：那你想干什么呢？

弟弟：你们踢不踢足球？我
　　　　　 tī

　　　觉得踢足球最有意思。
　　　 juéde

大海：好，那我们去踢足球。

弟弟：走吧。

Part II

最好的办法是走路

　　我觉得喜欢运动的人都很健康。我爸爸妈妈都喜欢运动，他们常常
　　　　　　　　　　　　　　　 jiànkāng

一起打乒乓球，他们很健康。我也喜欢运动，常常和同学踢足球、打羽毛

球，有时候也去溜冰、跑步，我也很健康。我弟弟跟我们不一样，他不喜
　　　　　　　　　 liūbīng

欢运动，也不喜欢上体育课，他现在太胖了，还常常感冒。医生说，他的

运动太少了。医生还说，想健康，最好的办法是走路。现在，我和弟弟每
　　　　　shǎo　　　　　　　　　　　　　　bànfǎ　zǒu lù

天走路去学校。我希望弟弟能喜欢运动，我希望他健康。

Exercises

Read 1 *Read the following words and expressions and match them with the proper pictures.*

A 踢足球　　B 吃水果健康　　C 打羽毛球　　D 多　　E 少
F 好办法　　G 走路上学　　H 太胖了　　I 溜冰　　J 打篮球

....H....　....C....　....A....　....J....　....B....

....G....　....I....　....D....　....E....　....F....

Listen 2 *Listen to the recording and then choose the correct answer.*

1）你喜欢打＿＿＿＿＿吗？　　　　A 羽毛球　　　B 乒乓球

2）小雨，＿＿＿＿打网球吧！　　　A 去　　　　　B 来

3）我不会＿＿＿＿。　　　　　　　A 溜冰　　　　B 喝水

4）你＿＿＿＿这个游戏有意思吗？　A 觉得　　　　B 健康

5）你们＿＿＿＿足球？　　　　　　A 踢不踢　　　B 起不起

6）我觉得这是一个好＿＿＿＿。　　A 胖　　　　　B 办法

7）他常常＿＿＿＿去超市买东西。　A 走路　　　　B 开车

Listen 3 *Listen to the recording and then tick the correct box.*

A	B	C	D	E	F
doesn't like playing badminton	wants to go ice skating	likes playing football best	is very healthy	is lacking exercise	doesn't know a good way to handle it

	A	B	C	D	E	F
京京						
大海						
小雨						
大卫						
丽丽						
大海的哥哥						

Read 4 *Complete the sentences according to the pictures.*

①
A 你打不打_____？
A 羽毛球 B 足球

②
A 这只小狗_____。
A 太胖了 B 太少了

③
B 他们一起去_____。
A 走路 B 溜冰

④
A 他不胖，很_____。
A 健康 B 漂亮

⑤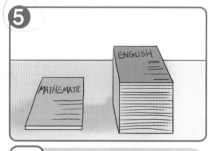
数学作业很_____。
A 多 B 少

⑥
A 来_____吧！
A 踢足球 B 打篮球

Read
5 *Read the following paragraph and answer the questions below in Chinese.*

　　我今年14岁，不高，可是（kěshì，but）很胖。我不喜欢运动，最不喜欢的科目是体育课。我常常感冒，医生说，我现在不太健康，因为我运动太少了。他说，他有一个好办法，就是给我一张运动时间表：每天早上走路去学校，下午放学走路回家。星期六去溜冰，或者（huòzhě，or）去踢足球，或者打羽毛球。我觉得他的办法不太好，可是我也没有好办法。

Questions:

1) 　　How does the person in the paragraph describe himself?

tall but very fat

2) 　　Which subject does he dislike most?

PE

3) 　　What's his problem now?

he has a cold

4) 　　What's the reason for that according to the doctor?

because he does not do enough sport

5) 　　What kind of timetable did the doctor give him?

he has to walk to and from school, on fridays go ice skating or play football or play badminton

6) 　　What does he think of the doctor's idea?

he doesn't think it is good

Talk
6 *Talk with your partner about different sport activities in Chinese according to the pictures.*

Write 7 *Complete the sentences with the proper Chinese character.*

1）这只小猫很 胖 (pàng)，那只小狗不 胖 (pàng)。

2）你 踢 (tī) 不 踢 (tī) 足球?

3）他每天 走 路 (zǒu lù) 去学校。

4）你 觉 得 (juéde) 溜冰有意思吗?

5）我也没有好 办 法 (bànfǎ)。

Talk 8 *Answer the following questions in Chinese.*

1) What is Xiaoyu doing? 跑步
2) What is Mary going to do with her friend? 打羽毛球
3) What is Dahai doing? 打足球
4) What is the boy sitting at the stairs doing? How does he look? 他吃蛋糕，他是胖
5) Do you have any suggestions for that boy? 我觉得他吃健康
6) What kind of extracurricular activities are you interested in?
我的爱好是打网球和游泳。

Write 9 *Write the following Chinese characters.*

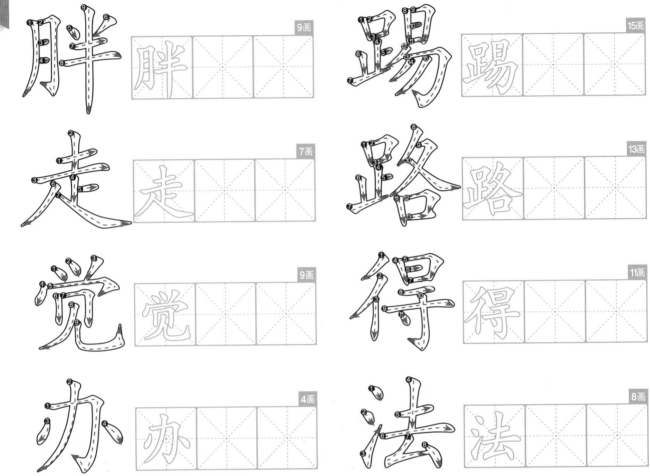

胖 9画
踢 15画
走 7画
路 13画
觉 9画
得 11画
办 4画
法 8画

Read 10 *Phonetics.*

歌谣(A Rhyme)
Gēyáo

大公鸡
Dà gōngjī

大公鸡，真美丽，红红的鸡冠花花衣。
Dà gōngjī, zhēn měilì, hóng hóng de jīguān huā huā yī.

每天清早喔喔啼，它叫我们早早起。
Měi tiān qīngzǎo wō wō tí, tā jiào wǒmen zǎo zǎo qǐ.

文化常识 *Cultural Tip*

孔子

　　孔子（公元前551年～公元前479年）是中国古代春秋时期最伟大的思想家和教育家，儒家学派创始人。孔子的思想主要见于《论语》一书。他创立的儒家思想对中国乃至世界都有深远的影响。

Confucius

Confucius (551 – 479 BC) was the greatest thinker and educationalist in ancient China, and the founder of Confucianism. His thoughts and teachings can be found in *The Analects of Confucius*. Confucianism exerts a far-reaching influence on both China and the rest of the world.

第四单元小结　Unit Four Summary

1 某人＋时间名词＋上＋了＋什么＋课？ Sb. + time + have + auxiliary word 了 + what + lessons?	你今天上了什么课？ What lessons have you had today? 大海昨天上了什么课？ What lessons did Dahai have yesterday?
2 某人＋时间名词＋上＋了＋某课程。 Sb. + time + have + auxiliary word 了 + a certain lesson.	我今天上了体育课。 I had a PE lesson today. 姐姐星期三上了音乐课。 The elder sister had a music lesson on Wednesday.
3 某人＋时间名词＋有/上＋什么课？ Sb. + time + have + what lessons?	你明天有什么课？ What lessons do you have tomorrow? 哥哥星期一上什么课？ What lessons does the elder brother have on Monday?
4 某人＋时间名词＋有/上＋某课程。 Sb. + time + have + certain lessons.	我明天有汉语课。 I have Chinese lessons tomorrow. 他星期一上地理课。 He has geography lessons on Monday.
5 主语＋难＋不＋难？ Subject + difficult + not + difficult?	汉语难不难？ Is Chinese difficult? 游泳难不难？ Is swimming difficult?
6 主语＋不＋难。 Subject + not + difficult.	汉语不难。 Chinese is not difficult. 打乒乓球不难。 Playing table tennis is not difficult.
7 什么＋名词＋最＋有意思/有趣？ What + noun + most + interesting?	什么课程最有趣？ What is the most interesting subject? 什么运动最有意思？ What is the most interesting sport?
8 某人＋最＋喜欢＋名词。 Sb. + most + like + noun.	我最喜欢历史。 History is my favourite subject. 哥哥最喜欢地理。 Geography is the elder brother's favourite subject.

9 主语＋太＋形容词＋了。 Subject + too +objective + auxiliary word 了.	你太胖了。 You're too fat. 法文考试太难了。 The French examination was too difficult.
10 来／去＋（某地）＋动词＋宾语（＋吧）！ Come/go + (some place) + verb + object (+ auxiliary word 吧)!	来打乒乓球吧！ Come and play table tennis! 去看电影吧！ Go and watch a film!
11 某人＋来／去＋动词＋宾语。 Sb. + come/go + verb + object.	我们去打羽毛球。 Let's go and play badminton. 大家来上中文课。 Everyone comes to a Chinese lesson.
12 某人＋动词＋不＋动词＋宾语？ Sb. + verb + not + verb + object?	你们踢不踢足球？ Do you play football? 爸爸喝不喝咖啡？ Does your dad drink coffee?
13 因为＋某人＋喜欢＋××，所以＋某人＋动词＋××。 Because + sb. + like + ××, so + sb. + verb + ××.	因为他喜欢运动，所以他喜欢体育课。 He likes doing sports, so he enjoys PE lessons. 因为姐姐喜欢音乐，所以她常常去听音乐会。 The elder sister likes music, so she goes to concerts quite a lot.

第十三课 *Lesson*

13

There Is a Football Match This Afternoon
今天下午有足球比赛

Learning Objectives

交际话题 Topic of conversation:

比赛信息
Bǐsài xìnxī
Match Information

基本句型 Sentence patterns:

她的表演好极了！　她是亚洲的。
因为我们今天有课，所以不能去。
学溜冰的时候，我很努力。

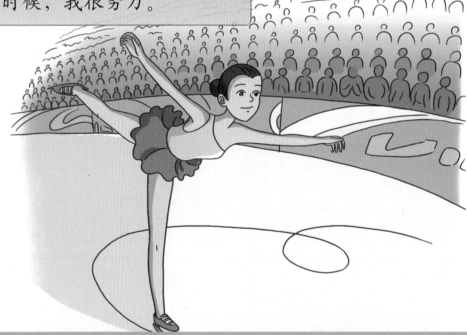

New Words

1. 队员 duìyuán　**n.** member of a (sport) team
2. 问 wèn　**v.** to ask
3. 为什么 wèishénme　**adv.** why
4. 打 dǎ　**v.** to make a phone call; to beat
5. 时间 shíjiān　**n.** time
6. 告诉 gàosù　**v.** to tell
7. 运动员 yùndòngyuán　**n.** sportsman
8. ...极了... jí le　extremely
9. 小时 xiǎoshí　**n.** hour
10. 时候 shíhou　**conj.** when, during, while
11. 累 lèi　**adj.** tired
12. 下 xià　**adj./prep./v.** next; under, below; to go down

Text

Part I

（在校园里）

大海：京京，你有天天的电话号码
　　　吗？

京京：我有他的电话号码。怎么了？

大海：今天下午有足球比赛，我们
　　　还少一个队员，我想问他
　　　　　　duìyuán　　　wèn
　　　有时间来踢足球吗。
　　　　　shíjiān

京京：他今天不能踢足球。

大海：为什么？

京京：因为我们今天有课，所以不
　　　能去。明天去，好吗？

大海：明天我们没有比赛了。

京京：我有办法。我给大卫打电
　　　　　　　　　　　　　dǎ

话。他今天下午没有课。

大海：他踢得好吗？

京京：我常常看他踢球，他踢得
　　　很好。

大海：我们下午三点开始比赛，在
　　　学校的运动场。

京京：好，我告诉他。
　　　　　gàosù

Part II

她的表演好极了

　　昨天我去市中心的体育馆看溜冰表演了。体育馆里看表演的人很多。表演
的运动员有二十多个，有美国的、法国的、德国的，也有英国的和中国的。
　yùndòngyuán

有一个女运动员是我最喜欢的，她是亚洲的，她很漂亮，表演好极了！现在我
They hade one female athlete who was she was Asian she was very the performane now I
my favourite beautiful was extremely good!

也在学溜冰，每个星期日去体育馆学习三个小时，很有趣。在那里我有很多新
also learning to every sunday I go to the gym and xiǎoshí it is very I now have a lot of new
iceskate practice for 3 hours fun

朋友。因为我也想跟那个运动员一样，所以学溜冰的时候，我很努力，不觉得
friends because I also want to practice with shíhou
there. professional athlete

累。下星期我们有一个小比赛，你想来看看吗?
lèi xià

Exercises

Read
1 *Read the following words and expressions and then match them with the proper pictures.*

A 高兴极了　　　B 篮球队员　　　C 游泳运动员　　　D 告诉
E 下个周末　　　F 一个小时　　　G 跑得很累　　　H 为什么

B

A

H

C

D

G

E

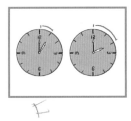
F

Listen
2 *Listen to the recording and then choose the correct answer.*

1) 他哥哥是＿＿＿＿＿＿。　　　　　　A 羽毛球队员　　B 羽毛球运动员

2) 我们＿＿＿个星期有考试。　　　　　A 上　　　　　　B 下

3) 他请了＿＿＿＿＿假。　　　　　　　A 一个小时　　　B 一个星期

4) 今天他不能来，＿＿＿＿＿他感冒了。　A 因为　　B 所以

5) 今天的作业多极了，我们都很＿＿＿＿＿。　A 累　　　　B 高兴

Listen 3 *Tick the correct box according to the recording.*

A	B	C	D	E	F
thinks today's history lesson was so boring	so tired	wants to be a member of the swimming team	will have an exam next week	studied for half an hour	missed the lesson due to illness

	A	B	C	D	E	F
玛丽						
大海						
小雨						
大卫						
丽丽						
本						

Read 4 *Complete the sentences according to the pictures.*

1

Ⓐ 我们踢了两个小时足球，_____。

A 累极　　**B** 高兴极了

2

Ⓐ 这个星期五不能比赛，___有考试。

A 因为　　**B** 所以

3 2011

Ⓑ 他学习了_____汉语。

A 一个小时　**B** 一个星期

4

医院在_____。

 这里　 那里

⑤ 他是_____。

Ⓐ 亚洲的　Ⓑ 美国的

⑥ 女孩子在_____舞蹈。

Ⓐ 表演　Ⓑ 告诉

Read 5 *Read the following paragraph and answer the questions below in Chinese.*

　　下个星期我们和新亚学校有篮球比赛。因为这个比赛，所以我和篮球队的队员们每个星期一、星期三、星期五的下午要打两个小时篮球。我们都很努力，也不觉得累。我们觉得我们能打得比新亚的队员好。下个星期你们也来学校的运动场看比赛吧，那里会有很多人，很热闹，因为我们的爸爸妈妈、同学都会去。

Questions:

1) *What is going to be on next week?*

a basketball match against a new Asian school

2) *What do they do to get ready?*

they play for 2 hours on Monday, Wednesday & Friday

3) *Why didn't they feel tired?*

4) *What do they think about their level?*

5) *What is going to take place on the playground of the school next week?*

6) *Who is going to the school to watch the match?*

Talk **6**

Talk about the tennis match in Chinese according to the poster.

Write **7**

Complete the sentences with the proper Chinese characters.

1）我的考试成绩不太好，（yīnwèi）考试太难了。

2）我头疼，（suǒyǐ）我想请假。

3）今天的比赛热闹（jí）了。

4）我打了一个下午的篮球，很（lèi），我想休息。

5）今天的作业我们做了一个（xiǎoshí）。

Talk **8**

Answer the following questions in Chinese.

1）Whom is this message for?

2）What's the problem with today's tennis class? Why?

3）When will the next class be held?

Write 9 *Write the following Chinese characters.*

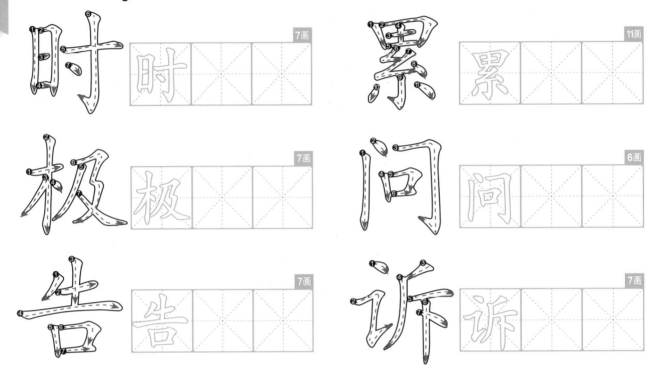

Read 10 *Phonetics.*

古诗(A Classical Poem)
Gǔshī

渡汉江
Dù Hàn Jiāng

唐 · 李频
Táng · Lǐ Pín

岭外音书绝，经冬复立春。
Lǐng wài yīn shū jué, jīng dōng fù lì chūn

近乡情更怯，不敢问来人。
Jìn xiāng qíng gèng qiè, bù gǎn wèn lái rén.

第十四课 *Lesson* **14**

Let's Watch Beijing Opera at the Theatre
我们去剧院看京剧吧

Learning Objectives

交际话题 Topic of conversation:

表演信息
Biǎoyǎn xìnxī
Show Information

基本句型 Sentence patterns:

我爸爸和妈妈都喜欢看京剧。
我跟爸爸一样，也会唱京剧。
去剧院看京剧吧。

New Words

1. 票 piào n. ticket
2. 久 jiǔ adv. for a long time
3. 总是 zǒngshì adv. always
4. 当然 dāngrán adv. of course; sure
5. 剧院 jùyuàn n. theatre
6. 售票处 shòupiàochù n. ticket office
7. 特别 tèbié adj. special
8. 订 dìng v. to book, to order
9. 晚 wǎn n./adj. evening, night; late
10. 早 zǎo n./adj. morning; early
11. 可是 kěshì conj. but, however
12. 京剧 jīngjù n. Beijing Opera
13. 故事 gùshi n. story

Text

Part I

（在网上聊天）

大卫： 你有下星期流行音乐表演的票吗？
票 piào

小雨： 没有。你想看这个表演，是吗？

大卫： 当然，我想看这个表演很久了。
当然 dāngrán   久 jiǔ

小雨： 流行音乐表演的票总是很难买，我也想买。
总是 zǒngshì

大卫： 你去附近剧院的售票处了吗？
剧院 jùyuàn   售票处 shòupiàochù

小雨： 我不去售票处买，在那里买

票的人特别多。我上网订票。
特别 tèbié   订 dìng

大卫： 怎么样？票没有了吗？

小雨： 没有了，我订得太晚了。
晚 wǎn

大卫： 以后，我们要早订票。
以后 yǐhòu   早 zǎo

小雨： 京京买了一张，她很高兴。
张 zhāng

大卫： 我看新闻了，有很多有名的演员来表演，我很想去看看。

小雨： 没有票，我们看电视吧。

大卫： 可是在电视上看跟在表演的
可是 kěshì
地方看不一样！

Part II

我们去剧院看京剧吧

你知道我在看什么吗？我在看京剧。我爸爸和妈妈都喜欢看京剧，
京剧 jīngjù

我爸爸还会唱京剧。我跟爸爸一样，也会唱。很多人觉得京剧很难，因为京剧里有很多中国历史故事，表演、音乐很不一样。因为我对京剧和中国历史都有兴趣，所以不觉得难。在我们这里的剧院常常有京剧表演，下个星期六，就有从中国来的演员表演京剧。我们一起去剧院看京剧吧。

gùshi

Exercises

Read 1 *Read the following words and expressions and then match them with the proper pictures.*

A 看京剧   B 剧院   C 上网订票   D 看故事
F 总是头疼   G 特别高   H 售票处   I 买票

A

C

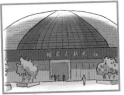
B

F

....

G

....

D

H

I

Listen 2 *Listen to the recording and then choose the correct answer.*

1) 他的英语说得＿＿＿＿＿＿好。   A 都   B 特别

2) 他们＿＿＿＿有考试。   A 没有   B 总是

3) 晚上他们去看＿＿＿＿。   A 京剧   B 剧院

4) 剧院的＿＿＿＿有一个购物中心。   A 附近   B 售票处

5) 爸爸妈妈买了＿＿＿＿。   A 一张票   B 一个京剧

Listen 3 *Listen to the recording and then tick the correct box.*

A	B	C	D	E	F
is interested in Beijing Opera	especially likes to talk	always coughs	went to the supermarket near the theatre	plays tennis for a long time	all his family members like the sportsman

	A	B	C	D	E	F
大海						
大卫						
京京						
小雨						
玛丽						
丽丽						

Read 4 *Complete the sentences according to the pictures.*

①  我们买了_____。
A 一张票　B 一个京剧表演

②  爸爸在_____。
A 售票处　B 剧院

③  他_____喜欢京剧。
A 不　B 特别

④  剧院在市中心的____。
A 附近　B 很远

⑤  他等了_____。
A 很久　B 总是

⑥  爸爸会_____。
A 唱京剧　B 打乒乓球

Read **5** *Read the following paragraph and answer the questions below in Chinese.*

　　2008年，爸爸去中国旅行，他在北京看了京剧。他很喜欢京剧，所以买了京剧的DVD给我。我和妈妈、弟弟一起看了DVD，我们都说我们不知道那个演员在唱什么。我问爸爸，爸爸说："我也听不懂，可是我觉得演员唱得很好听，他们的衣服很漂亮。"下个月剧院有一个京剧表演，我要和爸爸再去看。

Questions:

1)　　*What did the father do in Beijing?*

....

2)　　*Why did he buy the narrator a DVD?*

....

3)　　*How do the family members feel about the DVD?*

....

4)　　*How does the father feel about the performance?*

....

5)　　*What are they going to do next week?*

....

Talk **6** *Talk about the pictures in Chinese.*

Write
7
Complete the sentences with the proper Chinese characters.

1）爸爸妈妈要看电影，我去 订 票 （dìng piào）。

2）他病了，☐ ☐ （zǒngshì）咳嗽。

3）电影院在广场的 附 近 （fùjìn）。

4）我 ☐ ☐ （hěn jiǔ）没有给他写邮件了。

5）那个购物中心 特 别 （tèbié）漂亮。

Talk
8
Answer the following questions in Chinese.

1） *Where are the people now?*
2） *What do they want to do?*
3） *What's the reason for the long queue?*
4） *Do you think it's normal? Why?*

Write 9 Write the following Chinese characters.

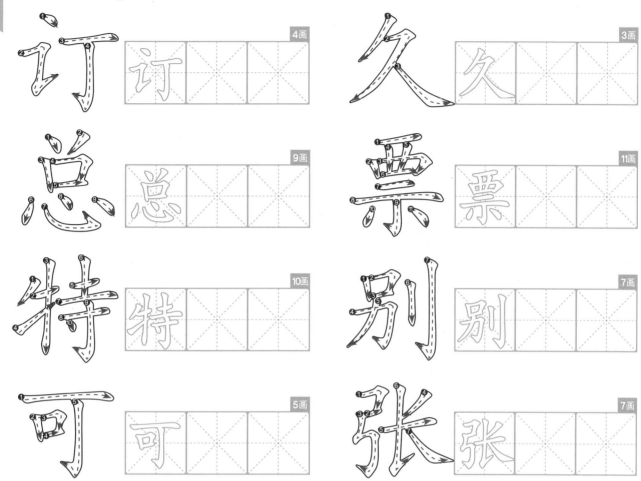

订 4画
久 3画
总 9画
票 11画
特 10画
别 7画
可 5画
张 7画

Read 10 Phonetics.

绕口令(A Tongue Twister)
Ràokǒulìng

大小与多少
Dàxiǎo yǔ duōshǎo

一个大，一个小，一只老虎一只猫。
Yí gè dà,　yí gè xiǎo,　yì zhī láohǔ yì zhī māo.

一个多，一个少，一群大雁一只鸟。
Yí gè duō,　Yí gè shǎo.　yì qún dàyàn yì zhī niǎo.

数一数，瞧一瞧，大小多少记得牢。
Shǔ yi shǔ,　qiáo yi qiáo,　dà xiǎo duō shǎo jì de láo.

第十五课 Lesson **15**

There Is a Good View Around Our House
我家的附近很漂亮

Learning Objectives

交际话题 Topic of conversation:

自然景物
Zìrán jǐngwù
Natural Scenery

基本句型 Sentence patterns:

北边的山跟西边的山一样高。
跑上山去。
跑上去，走下来。

New Words

1 近 jìn **adj.** near
2 山 shān **n.** mountain
3 条 tiáo **m.w.** (a measure word used for long narrow things like rivers, roads, etc.)
4 河 hé **n.** river
5 树 shù **n.** tree
6 草 cǎo **n.** grass, straw
7 花 huā **n.** flower
8 过 guò **v.** to cross; to go through; to experience; to live
9 上去 shàngqù **v.** to go up
10 下来 xiàlái **v.** to come down
11 天 tiān **n.** sky, weather, day
12 黑 hēi **adj.** black, dark

Text

Part I

（在街边饮品店）

小雨：明天的天气怎么样？

京京：我听了天气预报，明天下

雨，天气也很冷。

小雨：太不好了。

京京：为什么？

小雨：我想明天上午和你一起打

网球。

京京：不能在外边玩，我们一起去

体育馆打羽毛球吧。

小雨：去哪个体育馆？

京京：学校对面那个体育馆好吗？

小雨：从我家到那个体育馆很远。

京京：去市中心的体育馆呢？

小雨：那个体育馆很近，我坐

jìn

公共汽车去。

京京：我们明天上午十点见。

小雨：好。我们先打羽毛球，再

firstly ~ *again*

到旁边的购物中心和广场

去玩。

Part II

我家的附近很漂亮

我家不在市中心，从我家到市中心很远。我家的北边和西边都有

my house is not in the city centre, but it is far from my house to the city centre ~ *north and west of my house has*

山，北边的山跟西边的山一样高，西边的山下有一条小河，河的两边都

shān *north the mountain* *west the mountain* *tiáo* *hé* *on the river two banks*

mountains, *the north east mountain and the same height, the water* *mountains have one* *small river,*

是大树和草，那里还有很多花。我常常和朋友们过河，跑上山去。我们
跑上去，走下来，玩得很高兴，可是有些累。我们常常在天黑的时候回
家。我听了天气预报，下个星期日的天气很好，是晴天，不冷，也不
热。我和同学们要一起去我家附近的山上玩。

Exercises

Read 1 Read the following words and expressions and then match them with the proper pictures.

A 看天气预报　　B 一条河　　　C 天黑了　　　D 漂亮的花
E 高山　　　　　F 上山　　　　G 下山　　　　H 过河

....　　...............　　...............　　...............

....　　...............　　...............　　...............

Listen 2 Listen to the recording and then choose the correct answer.

1）我们跑＿＿＿＿＿＿山去。　　　　A 上　　　　B 下

2）他们走＿＿＿＿山来。　　　　　　A 上　　　　B 下

3）他家的附近有＿＿＿＿＿。　　　　A 花　　　　B 河

4）今天的＿＿＿＿怎么样?　　　　　A 天气　　　B 天黑

5）我们过＿＿＿＿去玩吧。　　　　　A 河　　　　B 山

Listen 3 *Listen to the recording and then tick the correct box.*

	A	B	C	D	E	F
A always go to the other side of the river	**B** likes flowers	**C** lives down the hill	**D** watches the weather forecast every day	**E** goes up the hill with classmates	**F** wants to have a rest because it's getting dark outside	

	A	B	C	D	E	F
天天						
大海和弟弟						
小雨						
玛丽						
大卫						
丽丽						

Read 4 *Complete the sentences according to the pictures.*

1

他们都在＿＿的旁边玩。

A 河　　**B** 山

2

他走＿＿山＿＿。

A 上，去　　**B** 下，来

3

他们在山＿＿＿＿＿。

A 上　　**B** 下

4

那里有山有＿＿＿＿。

A 河　　**B** 花

5

哥哥跑＿＿山＿＿。

A 上，去　　**B** 下，来

6

我的家旁边是＿＿＿＿。

A 大河　　**B** 学校

Read
5

Read the following paragraph and answer the questions below in Chinese.

　　我爷爷今年70岁了，他非常健康。他家在山下，那里有一条河，河的两边有很多花，很漂亮。他每天早上走路上山。我和弟弟常常去他家玩，我们喜欢和他聊天儿，听他说，他在学校里怎么教书、他的学生们怎么样。

Questions:

1)　　Who is the narrator talking about?

....

2)　　How about the person's health?

....

3)　　How's the view around the person's house?

....

4)　　What does the person do every morning?

....

5)　　What do they often talk about?

....

Read
6

Talk about the pictures in Chinese.

Write 7 *Complete the sentences with the proper Chinese characters.*

1）他家的附近有一条 ☐（hé）。

2）天 ☐（hēi）了， 我们不玩了。

3）你看今天的天气 ☐☐（yùbào）了吗？有雪吗？

4）他们都上 ☐（shān）了，我们也上去吧。

5）你喜欢什么 ☐（huā）？红的还是粉红的？

Talk 8 *Answer the following questions in Chinese.*

1）Where do they live?

2）What is at the foot of the hill?

3）Where is their shool? How do they go to school?

4）What can they do opposite their house?

Write
9 *Write the following Chinese characters.*

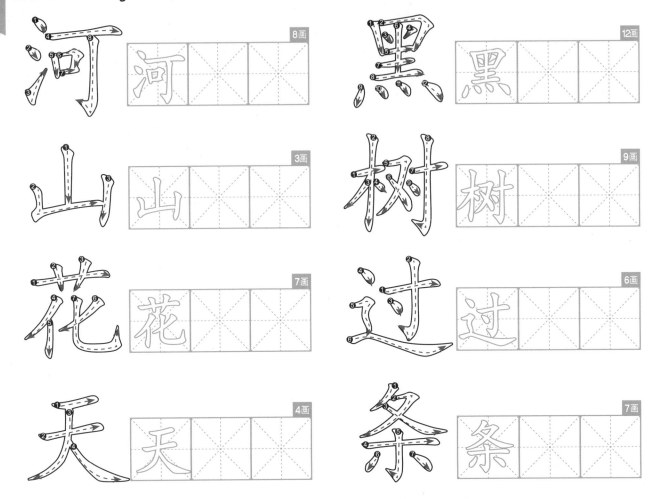

Read
10 *Phonetics.*

歌谣(A Rhyme)
Gēyáo

小画笔
Xiǎo huàbǐ

画苹果，苹果香。
Huà píngguǒ , píngguǒ xiāng .

画小鸟，小鸟唱。
Huà xiǎo niǎo , xiǎo niǎo chàng .

画星星，星星亮。
Huà xīngxing , xīngxing liàng .

小画笔，你真棒。
Xiǎo huàbǐ , nǐ zhēn bàng .

京剧脸谱

　　京剧脸谱是京剧具有民族特色的一种特殊的化妆方法，是分类型地用不同色彩来表现某种性格的人物。一般来说，红色脸谱表示忠勇，黑色的脸谱表示正直、勇猛，黄色的脸谱表示凶狠，蓝色或绿色的脸谱表示一些刚强、粗犷，白色的脸谱一般象征阴险狡诈等等。

Beijing Opera Masks

The types of masks in Beijing Opera are the result of unique facial makeup depicting different characters and remarkable images through the use of certain different colours. Generally speaking, red indicates devotion and loyalty. Black symbolizes courage, bravery and uprightness. Yellow signifies fierceness. A blue or green face tells the audience that the character represents staunchness and roughness. White suggests sinisterness and craftiness.

第五单元小结　Unit Five Summary

1 主语＋形容词＋极了！ Subject + adjective + auxiliary word极了！	他的表演好极了！ His performance was great! 市中心热闹极了！ The city centre is lively!
2 某人＋是＋某地＋的。 Sb. + is + somewhere + auxiliary word的.	他是亚洲的。 He is Asian. 这个运动员是欧洲的。 This athlete is European.
3 时间名词＋有＋某活动。 Time + have + a certain activity.	今天下午有足球比赛。 There is a football match this afternoon. 这个星期有流行音乐表演。 Thcre is a pop concert this week.
4 因为＋某人＋日期$_1$＋动词（＋宾语），所以日期$_2$＋动词（＋宾语）。 Because + sb. + date$_1$ + verb + object, so + date$_2$ + verb+(object).	因为我们今天有课，所以不能去。 Because we have classes today, we have to play badminton tomorrow. 因为弟弟今天有考试，所以星期天去游泳。 Because the younger brother has an exam today, he has to go swimming on Sunday.
5 某人$_1$＋和＋某人$_2$＋都＋喜欢＋动词＋宾语。 Sb.$_1$ + and + sb.$_2$ + both + like + verb + object.	爸爸和妈妈都喜欢看京剧。 Dad and mum both like watching Beijing Opera. 我和弟弟都喜欢听音乐。 My younger brother and I both like listening to music.
6 某人$_1$＋跟＋某人$_2$＋一样，也＋动词＋宾语。 Sb.$_1$ + and + sb.$_2$ + the same, also + verb + object.	我跟爸爸一样，也喜欢京剧。 I like Beijing Opera and so does my dad. 我跟老师一样，也学习太极拳。 I study *Tai chi chuan* and so does the teacher.
7 （主语＋一起）＋去＋某处＋动词＋宾语＋吧。 (Subject+ together) + go + somewhere + verb + object + auxiliary word吧.	去剧院看京剧吧。 Let's go and watch Beijing Opera at the theatre. 去市中心买书吧。 Let's go and buy books in the city centre.

第五单元小结	**Unit Five Summary**

7 某处₁+的+名词+跟+某处₂+的（+名词）+一样+形容词。 Somewhere₁ + auxiliary word的 + noun + and + somewhere₂ + auxiliary word的 (+noun)+ same + adjective.	北边的山跟西边的（山）一样高。 The mountain in the north is as high as the mountain in the west. 学校的电脑跟家里的（电脑）一样好。 The computers at school are as good as my computer at home.
8 动词+上／下+某处+来／去。 Verb + up/down + somewhere + come/go.	跑上山去。 Run up the hill. 走下楼来。 Go downstairs.
9 动词₁+上去，动词₂+下来。 Verb₁ + up, verb₂ + down.	跑上去，走下来。 Run up and then walk down. 骑上去，跑下来。 Ride up and then run down.

第十六课 Lesson **16**

There Are Many Places to Have Fun in Beijing
北京有很多好玩的地方

Learning Objectives

交际话题 Topic of conversation:
城市和景点
Chéngshì hé jǐngdiǎn
Cities and Sights

基本句型 Sentence patterns:
北京快到了。
你没去过北京吧?
我看过明信片,可是没去过。
上海比南京大。

New Words

1 快…了 kuài...le soon; about to
2 过 guò **part.** (used after a verb to indicate a past action or state)
3 城市 chéngshì **n.** city
4 风景 fēngjǐng **n.** scenery
5 故宫 Gùgōng **n.** the Forbidden City
6 长城 Chángchéng **n.** the Great Wall
   长 cháng **adj.** long

7 哈哈 hāhā **n.** (an exclamation used to express triumph or satisfaction)
8 南京 Nánjīng **n.** Nanjing
9 明信片 míngxìnpiàn **n.** postcard
10 春天 chūntiān **n.** spring
11 夏天 xiàtiān **n.** summer
12 秋天 qiūtiān **n.** fall, autumn
13 冬天 dōngtiān **n.** winter

Text

Part I

（本和他的父母在飞机上）

本：　爸爸，北京快到了。你没去
　　　kuài　le
　　　过北京吧？
　　　guò

爸爸：没去过。我在电视上看过这个
　　　城市 的风景。
　　　chéngshì　fēngjǐng.

本：　我也在电视上看过。北京是
　　　中国最大的城市。

妈妈：北京最有名的地方是故宫、
　　　　　　　　　　　　　　　Gùgōng
　　　长城，你知道吗？
　　　Chángchéng

本：　我当然知道了。

爸爸：故宫怎么样呢？

本：　它很大，很漂亮……

妈妈：长城呢？

本：　它很长……
　　　cháng

妈妈：哈哈！你知道得很多呢！
　　　hāhā

本：　我还知道上海和南京。
　　　　　　　　　　　Nánjīng

妈妈：这两个城市都是中国的大城市，
　　　上海比南京大。我们也要去看
　　　看。你一定会喜欢的。

本：　我要买很多中国风景的明信片
　　　　　　　　　　　　　　　míngxìnpiàn
　　　给我的同学。

Part II

北京有很多好玩的地方

二〇〇九年我去过北京。北京的春天风很大。夏天从六月开始，天气
　　　　　　　　　　　　　　　　chūntiān　　　　　　xiàtiān

特别热。秋天是从九月到十一月，这个时候天气最好，风景最漂亮，很
　　　qiūtiān

多人喜欢去山上玩。北京的冬天(dōngtiān)很冷。你看，我有很多北京冬天的明信片。这是故宫，我和爸爸妈妈在故宫里走了一天，因为那里太大了，所以我们非常累。这是冬天的长城，漂亮吧？北京还有很多好玩的地方，我看过明信片，可是没去过，我还想再去北京。

Exercises

1 Read Read the following words and expressions and then match them with the proper pictures.

A 故宫　　B 长城　　C 上海的风景　D 明信片
E 春天的花　F 夏天的雨　G 秋天的风　　H 冬天非常冷

2 Listen Listen to the recording and then choose the correct answer.

1）_____快来了。　　　　A 春天　　B 秋天

2）这里的_____非常冷。　　　　A 秋天　　B 冬天

3）我看过南京的_____。　　　A 电影　　B 明信片

4）我觉得上海的_____非常漂亮。A 地方　　B 风景

5）我去过_____。　　　　　　A 长城　　B 故宫

Listen 3 *Listen to the recording and then tick the correct box.*

A	B	C	D	E	F
hasn't been to the Forbidden City	is eager to go to the Great Wall	bought many postcards of Nanjing	likes the view from the mountain very much	is not very happy that spring is coming	plans to go travelling during the winter vacation

	A	B	C	D	E	F
京京						
大海						
小雨						
大卫						
丽丽						
本						

Read 4 *Complete the sentences according to the pictures.*

1 火车＿＿＿＿到上海了。
A 快　　**B** 太

2 ＿＿＿＿下雨了。
A 非常　　**B** 快

3 她＿＿＿＿北京。
A 去过　　**B** 去过没

4 我＿＿＿＿京剧。
A 看过　　**B** 没看过

5 这是一＿＿＿＿上海的明信片。
A 条　　**B** 张

Read
5

Read the following paragraph and answer the questions below in Chinese.

　　这个夏天爸爸有十天假，我们去了中国上海。以前 (yǐqián, before) 我没去过上海，我看过上海的明信片，非常喜欢这个城市。上海的夏天热极了，我们总是喝水。我们去了很多漂亮的地方，吃了很多好吃的东西，我觉得那里吃的东西非常便宜。

Questions:

1)　　When did they go to Shanghai?

....

2)　　Has he been to Shanghai before? How did he know about this city?

....

3)　　What is Shanghai's summer like?

....

4)　　What did they do in Shanghai?

....

5)　　What does he think about the price of food in Shanghai?

....

Talk
6

Talk about the four seasons according to the pictures.

Write 7 *Complete the sentences with the proper Chinese characters.*

1) 上海是一个非常热闹的 ☐ ☐ (chéngshì)。

2) 春天的 ☐ ☐ (fēngjǐng) 特别漂亮。

3) 我买了长城的 ☐ ☐ ☐ (míngxìnpiàn)。

4) 那个城市的 ☐ ☐ (xiàtiān) 热不热？

5) 冬天 ☐ (kuài) 到了。

Talk 8 *Look at the pictures and answer the following questions in Chinese.*

1) How many seasons are there in the pictures? What are they?
2) How is the weather in each season?
3) What do people do in each season? Do you think these activities are interesting or not?

Write 9 *Write the following Chinese characters.*

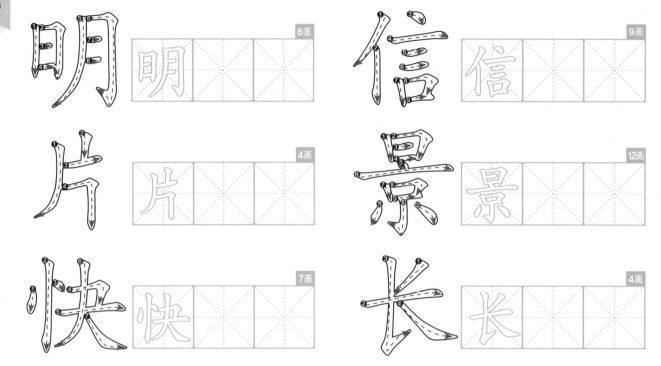

Read 10 *Phonetics.*

孔子语录(Confucius Quotes)
Kǒngzǐ yǔlù

论语·为政
Lúnyǔ · wéi zhèng

春秋时期·孔子
Chūnqiū shíqī · Kǒngzǐ

子曰："学而不思则罔，思而不学则殆。"
Zǐ yuē:　"Xué ér bù sī zé wǎng,　sī ér bù xué zé dài."

子曰："温故而知新，可以为师矣。"
Zǐ yuē:　"Wēn gù ér zhī xīn,　kéyǐ wéi shī yǐ."

第十七课 Lesson 17

Chinese Festivals Are Great Fun
中国的节日很有趣

Learning Objectives

交际话题 Topic of conversation:
节日和习俗
Jiérì hé xísú
Festivals and Customs

基本句型 Sentence patterns:
春节是中国最重要的节日。
饺子很好吃。
中秋节除了吃月饼，还吃水果。

New Words

1 月饼 yuèbǐng n. moon cake
2 中秋节 Zhōngqiū Jié n. the Mid-Autumn Festival
3 月亮 yuèliang n. moon
4 除了 chúle conj. except, besides
5 祝 zhù v. to bless, to wish
6 春节 Chūn Jié n. the Spring Festival
7 重要 zhòngyào adj. important
8 节日 jiérì n. festival
9 饺子 jiǎozi n. dumpling
10 晚会 wǎnhuì n. evening party
11 …的时候 …(de) shíhou conj. when…, at the time
12 活动 huódòng n. activity
13 舞龙 wǔ lóng to perform a dragon dance
14 舞狮 wǔ shī to perform a lion dance
15 人们 rénmen n. people

Text

Part I

（在京京家里，大卫和京京在看中国电视节目广告。）

大卫：这是什么？

京京：这是月饼。中秋节快到了，
yuèbǐng　Zhōngqiū Jié

中国人都要吃月饼。

大卫：中秋节是什么时候？

京京：每年中秋节的日子不一样，

常常在九月。

大卫：九月是秋天吗？

京京：是的，九月的天气最好，

不冷也不热。

大卫：中秋节你们做什么？

京京：和家里的人一起吃月饼、看月亮。
yuèliang

大卫：吃月饼？月饼好吃吗？

京京：好吃，我非常喜欢吃。中秋节

你来我家吃吧。

大卫：我太高兴了！

京京：我们家有一个新朋友，我们

也很高兴。

大卫：除了月饼，还有什么好吃的？
chúle

京京：中秋节除了吃月饼，我们还吃

水果。

大卫：中秋节我也做点心给你们吃。

京京：太好了！现在我先祝你中秋
zhù

节快乐！

Part II

春节是中国最重要的节日

春节是中国最重要的节日。每年春节的日子不一样，常常在一
Chūn Jié　　　　zhòngyào　　jiérì

月，今年的春节在二月。春节的时候人们常常是一家人在一起聊天儿、喝

de shíhòu

茶、听音乐、做饺子、看电视……人们都看春节晚会，因为有很多有名的

jiǎozi   rénmen   wǎnhuì

演员表演节目。晚上十二点我们吃饺子。你吃过饺子吗？饺子很好吃，我

最喜欢吃猪肉和蔬菜的饺子，我妹妹跟我不一样，她不喜欢饺子，她喜欢

蛋糕。春节的时候，外边还有很多有趣的活动，除了舞龙，还有舞狮，人

huódòng   wǔ lóng   wǔ shī

们都很喜欢看。

Exercises

Read 1 Match the English with the Chinese.

A 重要的考试   B 中秋节晚会   C 节目活动   D 吃饺子   E 买月饼
F 快到春节了   G 看舞龙   H 会舞狮   I 祝你健康

to buy moon cakes	festival activities	Mid-Autumn Festival TV Gala	the Spring Festival is coming	to watch dragon dance

to be able to do the lion dance	an important examination	May you have good health.	to eat dumplings

Listen 2 Listen to the recording and then choose the correct answer.

1）我们去看_____吧。   A 舞龙   B 舞狮

2）春节的时候，每家都吃_____。   A 饺子   B 月饼

3）中秋节有_____，还有水果。   A 饺子   B 月饼

4）节日的时候你有_____吗？   A 晚会   B 活动

5）这个电子邮件很_____。   A 重要   B 热闹

Listen 3 *Listen to the recording and then tick the correct box.*

A	B	C	D	E	F
likes to eat dumplings very much	hasn't had moon cake	will have an important test tomorrow	performed at a party	learns Chinese as well as Chinese history	wants to see the lion dance

	A	B	C	D	E	F
大卫想						
小雨						
大海喜欢						
丽丽学习						
京京有						
玛丽没有						

Read 4 *Complete the sentences according to the pictures.*

① 晚上除了鸡___有海鲜。
A 还　B 都

② 那个晚会很_____。
A 好看　B 好吃

③ _____你新年好！
A 想　B 祝

④ 过了春节_____就来了。
A 春天　B 冬天

⑤ 我们去看_____吧。
A 舞龙　B 舞狮

⑥ 中秋节吃_____！
A 月饼和水果　B 蛋糕和鲜花

Read 5 *Read the following paragraph and answer the questions below in Chinese.*

今年的春节我们在外边旅行，从我们的城市到那个地方很远。春节那里比我们的城市热闹。我们吃了很多没吃过的东西，除了吃，我们还看了那里的节日活动，我们对他们的活动特别有兴趣。

Questions:

1) Where were they during the Spring Festival?

....

2) Was the place far from their city?

....

3) What was the place like during the Spring Festival?

....

4) What did they do there?

....

5) What are they interested in?

....

Talk 6 *Talk about what these people are doing to celebrate the Spring Festival in Chinese according to the pictures.*

Write 7 *Complete the sentences with the proper Chinese characters.*

1）这是一个 ☐☐ （zhòngyào）的电话号码。

2）今天的 ☐☐ （huódòng）时间会很长，你们不要等我，

先休息吧。

3）你打算在 ☐☐ （wǎnhuì）上表演唱歌还是跳舞？

4）今天我们 ☐☐ （chúle）数学课，还有地理课。

5）☐ （zhù）你春节好！

Talk 8 *Look at the picture and answer the following questions in Chinese.*

1） Where are the people now?
2） What season is it? What time is it now?
3） How is the weather?
4） What are they doing?
5） What is there on the table?

Write 9 *Write the following Chinese characters.*

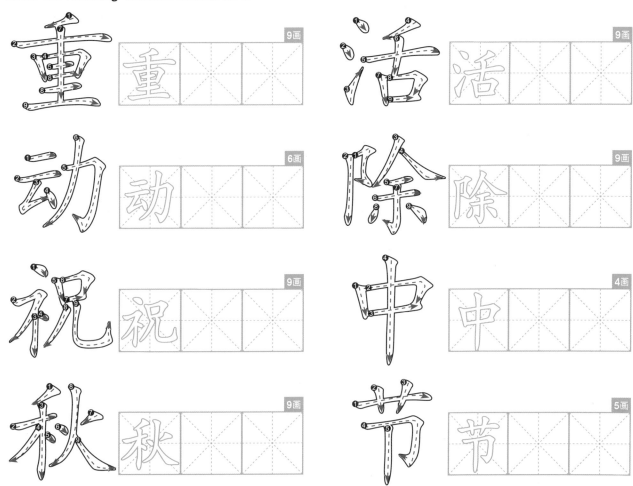

重　9画
动　6画
祝　9画
秋　9画
活　9画
除　9画
中　4画
节　5画

Read 10 *Phonetics.*

歌谣(A Rhyme)

人说山西好地方
Rén shuō Shānxī hǎo dìfang

人说山西好地方，　地肥水美五谷香。
Rén shuō Shānxī hǎo dìfang，　dì féi shuǐ měi　wúgǔ xiāng．

左手一指太行山，　右手一指是吕梁。
Zuǒshǒu yì zhǐ Tàiháng Shān，　yòushǒu yì zhǐ shì Lǚliáng．

第十八课 Lesson

18

We Celebrate Christmas Day at Home
我们在家庆祝圣诞节

Learning

交际话题 Topic of conversation:

节日计划
Jiérì jìhuà
Holiday Plans

基本句型 Sentence patterns:

他已经到北京了吗？他问我打算去哪里。
我们在家庆祝圣诞节。

New Words

1 对不起 duìbuqǐ I'm sorry; excuse me

2 没关系 méi guānxi it doesn't matter

3 已经 yǐjīng **adv.** already

4 新年 xīnnián **n.** New Year; New Year's Day

5 圣诞节 Shèngdàn Jié **n.** Christmas Day

6 庆祝 qìngzhù **v.** to celebrate

7 计划 jìhuà **n./v.** plan; to plan

8 旅行社 lǚxíngshè **n.** travel agency

9 希望 xīwàng **v./n.** to wish; wish

10 旅行团 lǚxíngtuán **n.** tour

11 星期 xīngqī **n.** week

12 滑雪 huáxuě **n.** skiing

13 参加 cānjiā **v.** to join in; to take part in

Text

Part I

（玛丽在家里和丽丽聊天儿，大海给玛丽打电话……）

玛丽：对不起，丽丽，是大海的电话。
　　　duìbuqǐ

丽丽：没关系。他已经到北京了吗？
　　　méi guānxi　yǐjīng

玛丽：是的，他已经在那里玩了

　　　三天了。

丽丽：今年新年他会在北京吗？
　　　　　xīnnián

玛丽：是的，他会在北京。

丽丽：他说什么了？

玛丽：圣诞节快到了，他问我打
　　　Shèngdàn Jié

　　　算去哪里。我说，我打算就

　　　在家里庆祝圣诞节。
　　　　　　qìngzhù

丽丽：你不去旅行吗？

玛丽：今年圣诞节我不想去。

　　　你呢？你有什么计划？
　　　　　　　　　　jìhuà

丽丽：我去问了一个旅行社，希望十
　　　　　　　　　lǚxíngshè　xīwàng

　　　二月参加去香港的旅行团。
　　　　　cānjiā

玛丽：他们有去香港的旅行团吗？

丽丽：有很多，五天的、一星期
　　　　　　　　　　　　　xīngqī

　　　的、十天的都有。

玛丽：你想去香港做什么？

丽丽：买东西！圣诞节的时候，那

　　　里的东西非常便宜。

Part II

我们在家庆祝圣诞节

今年的圣诞节我们学校有两个星期的假期。Mark计划和爸爸妈妈坐飞

机到中国旅行，除了去北京，他们也想去上海。大卫计划和爸爸开车去山上

滑雪。玛丽说她想跟朋友去吃饭、跳舞，庆祝圣诞节。丽丽说圣诞节的时候
huá xuě
外边太冷了，她想在家里玩电脑游戏！我觉得这些太没有意思了！我问了我
的弟弟，问他的同学们想做什么。弟弟说圣诞节的时候剧院有很多表演，他
打算和他的同学们去看表演。今年我打算在家庆祝圣诞节，爸爸妈妈已经买
了很多东西。我正在想，我给爸爸妈妈和弟弟买什么呢？

Exercises

Read 1 Match the English with the Chinese.

A 过圣诞节　　　B 十二月　　　C 庆祝春节　　　D 已经去过了

E 想吃蛋糕　　　F 学期计划　　　G 问老师　　　H 参加滑雪

to celebrate the Spring Festival	to want to have cakes	December	a plan for the school term
to celebrate Christmas	have already been there	to ask the teacher	to go on a skiing trip

Listen 2 Listen to the recording and then choose the correct answer.

1）下个星期我去＿＿＿＿＿＿。　　　A 旅行　　　B 旅行社

2）＿＿＿＿请你来我家。　　　A 中秋节　　　B 圣诞节

3）他＿＿＿＿＿＿去过北京。　　　A 没有　　　B 已经

4）我们＿＿＿＿＿＿就来了。　　　A 早　　　B 早上

5）我＿＿＿＿＿＿在家庆祝圣诞节。　　　A 计划　　　B 希望

Listen 3 Listen to the recording and then tick the correct box.

A	B	C	D	E	F
will go skiing in December	has already gone to the travel agency	asked the teacher about today's homework	wants to be a doctor in the future	celebrate Christmas Day together	has had a study plan

	A	B	C	D	E	F
小雨						
大卫						
京京						
丽丽						
大海						
May和朋友						

Read 4 Complete the sentences according to the pictures.

1 姐姐在_____。
A 旅行 B 旅行社

2 她____我累不累。
A 问 B 希望

3 晚饭_____做好了。
A 还 B 已经

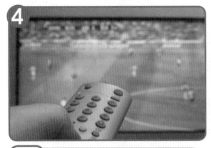
4 比赛_____开始了。
A 已经 B 没有

5 他____我将来想做什么。
A 计划 B 问

6 我_____参加游泳比赛。
A 计划 B 希望

Read
5

Read the following paragraph and answer the questions below in Chinese.

　　圣诞节快到了，我问爸爸这个圣诞节有什么活动。爸爸说今年圣诞节我们再去香港。我们去过香港，在那里玩了一个星期，香港在节日的时候很热闹，很好玩，也有很多好吃的，饺子啊、蛋糕啊，我太喜欢那个地方了。我非常高兴能在那里庆祝圣诞节。

Questions:

1)   What time is it now?

....

2)   Where are they going at Christmas?

....

3)   Have they been there before?

....

4)   How does he feel about the place?

....

5)   What is his wish?

....

Talk
6

Talk about this family's Christmas plans in Chinese according to the pictures.

Write 7 *Complete the sentences with the proper Chinese characters.*

1）我不希望参加 ☐ ☐ ☐ (lǚxíngshè) 旅行。

2）这个学期的 ☐ ☐ (jìhuà) 做好了吗？

3）我 ☐ (wèn) 老师周末有没有去 ☐ ☐ (huá xuě)。

4）他们的学校 ☐ ☐ (yǐjīng) 放假了。

5）今年你们打算怎么 ☐ ☐ (qìngzhù) 圣诞节？

Talk 8 *Look at the pictures and answer the following questions in Chinese.*

Snow Skiing Tour

发　团：周二/周五
行　程：4天
出　发：12月
目的地：哈尔滨
费　用：4480元/人

Beach Tour

发　团：周三/周六
行　程：4天
出　发：12月
目的地：海南岛
费　用：3480元/人

1）　*What is the season in December in your city?*

2）　*Can you go skiing now in your city?*

3）　*Can you go to the beach and swim now in your city?*

4）　*Between the two tours, Which one do you prefer?*

Write 9 *Write the following Chinese characters.*

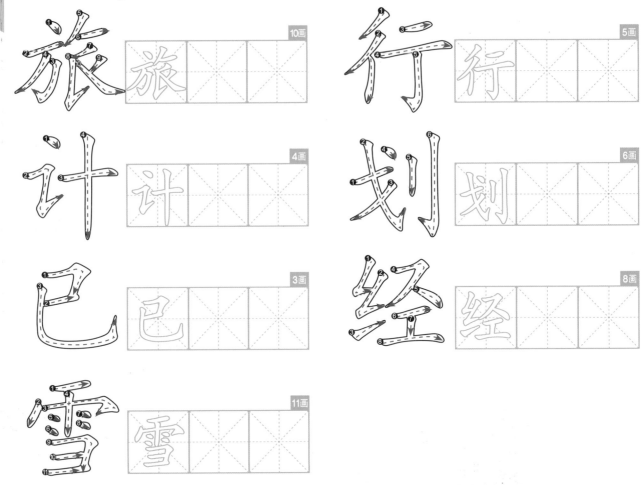

Read 10 *Phonetics.*

古诗(A Classical Poem)
Gǔshī

元日
Yuán rì

宋　·　王安石
Sòng　·　Wáng Ān shí

爆竹声中一岁除，春风送暖入屠苏，
Bàozhú shēng zhōng yí suì chú ，chūnfēng sòng nuǎn rù túsū ，

千门万户瞳瞳日，总把新桃换旧符。
qiān mén wàn hù tóng tóng rì ，zǒng bǎ xīn táo huàn jiù fú .

春节习俗

春节是中国最重要的节日之一，有许多来自古代的习俗，比如放鞭炮、守岁、长辈给晚辈压岁钱等等。春节时的一些活动都有喜庆的寓意，比如吃饺子意味着新旧交替，团圆美满；吃年糕表示生活甜蜜，一年更比一年好；贴春联、门神、"福"字是保佑家庭吉祥如意。

The Spring Festival Customs

The Spring Festival is the most important festival for the Chinese people. There are many ancient customs and traditions, such as setting off fireworks, staying up late to see the New Year in, receiving money in red paper envelopes from elders, etc. The traditions of the Spring Festival reflect the peoples' wishes for happiness in the coming year. For example, having dumplings means bidding farewell to the old and ushering in the new, as well as signifying family reunion and good luck. Having New Year cakes on this occasion represents the desire of

people to better themselves and rise "higher and higher, year after year". The hanging of Spring Festival couplets, pictures of the god of doors and the Chinese character "*fu*" are thought to bless families with peace and good luck.

第六单元小结　Unit Six Summary

1 某地＋快＋到＋了。 Somewhere + nearly + arrives + auxiliary word 了.	北京快到了。 We are pulling into Beijing now. 火车站快到了。 We are almost at the railway station.
2 某人＋（没）/去＋过＋某地＋吗? Sb. + (not)/have been to + somewhere + interrogative word ma 吗?	你去过故宫吗? Have you been to the Forbidden City? Jim没去过香港吗? Hasn't Jim been to Hong Kong?
3 某人＋去＋过＋某地。 Sb. + have been to + somewhere.	我去过故宫。 I have been to the Forbidden City. 他去过长城。 He has been to the Great Wall.
4 某人＋没＋去＋过＋某地。 Sb. + never + have been to + somewhere.	我没去过长城。 I have never been to the Great Wall. 弟弟没去过上海。 The younger brother has never been to Shanghai.
5 名词（词组）＋是＋某地＋最＋形容词＋的＋名词。 Noun (noun phrase) + is + somewhere + most + adjective + auxiliary word 的 + noun.	春节是中国最重要的节日。 The Spring Festival is the most important festival in China. 足球是英国最重要的运动。 Football is the most important sport in Britain.
6 某食品＋很＋好吃。 A certain food + very + delicious.	饺子很好吃。 Dumplings are delicious. 月饼很好吃。 Moon cakes are delicious.
7 主语＋很＋好看。 Subject + very + well performed.	春节晚会很好看。 The Spring Festival Gala was well performed. 舞狮很好看。 The lion dance was well performed.

8 某节日＋除了＋动词＋宾语₁，还＋动词＋宾语₂。 A certain festival + not only + verb + object₁, but also + verb + object₂.	中秋节除了吃月饼，还吃水果。 During the Mid-Autumn Festival, besides moon cakes, people can also eat fruit. 春节除了舞龙，还有舞狮。 Apart from dragon dances, there are also lion dances during the Spring Festival.
9 某人₁＋问＋某人₂＋动词＋疑问代词。 Sb.₁ + ask +sb.₂ + verb + interrogative word.	他问我去哪里。 He asked me where I am going. 弟弟问我写什么。 The younger brother asked what I am writing.
10 某人＋在＋某处（＋方位名词）＋动词＋宾语。 Sb. + at (in) + somewhere (+ direction) + verb + object.	我们在家里庆祝圣诞节。 We celebrate Christmas at home. 京京在图书馆里看书。 Jingjing reads books in the library.
11 某人＋已经＋到＋某地＋了＋吗? Sb. + already + arrive + somewhere + auxiliary word 了 + interrogative word 吗?	他已经到北京了吗? Has he already arrived in Beijing? 哥哥已经到英国了吗? Has the elder brother already arrived in Britain?

第十九课 *Lesson* **19**

The Spring Festival Gala Is Starting Soon on TV!
春节晚会快要开始了！

Learning Objectives

交际话题 Topic of conversation:
春节 晚会
Chūn Jié wǎnhuì
The Spring Festival Gala Show

基本句型 Sentence patterns:
春节晚会快要开始了！
每个节目都很好看。
杂技特别精彩。

New Words

1 欢迎 huānyíng **v.** to welcome
2 进 jìn **v.** to come in
3 开 kāi **v.** to turn on
4 快要 kuàiyào **adv.** soon; in no time
5 杂技 zájì **n.** acrobatics
6 精彩 jīngcǎi **adj.** brilliant, wonderful
7 其他 qítā **adj.** other
8 家人 jiārén **n.** family members
9 第 dì **pref.** (prefix for ordinal numbers)
10 次 cì **m.w.** times
11 包 bāo **v.** to wrap

Text

Part I

妈妈: 欢迎你, 本。请进! 天天在等你呢。
　　　huānyíng　　　　jìn

本: 谢谢!

妈妈: 天天, 电视开了吗?
　　　　　　　　kāi

天天: 开了, 妈妈。

妈妈: 本, 来看电视吧, 春节晚会快要
　　　　　　　　　　　　　　kuàiyào
　　　开始了! 你和我们一起看中国
　　　的春节晚会。

本: 好。今天的晚会有什么节目?

天天: 有唱歌、跳舞, 节目太多了,
　　　每个节目都很好看。

本: 有没有杂技? 我最喜欢杂技了。
　　　　　　zájì

天天: 我也喜欢。春节晚会上的杂技
　　　特别精彩。
　　　　　jīngcǎi

本: 你们看这个演员, 他去过美
　　　国, 我在美国看过他的表演。

天天: 春节晚会上都是很有名的演员。

妈妈: 节目预报说, 今年春节晚会上
　　　还有美国演员。

本: 是吗? 太好了。

妈妈: 本, 这是你第一次过春节吗?
　　　　　　　　　dì-yī cì

本: 是的, 我们不过春节。

天天: 中国的春节和你们的圣诞节一
　　　样, 都是很重要的节日。

Part II

在中国过春节

爸爸妈妈:

　　你们好!

　　我来中国一个星期了, 我去了上海、南京, 吃了很多好吃的东西。

Part II

现在我已经到北京了。我去了长城、故宫和一些其他的地方。这两个地
qítā

方都非常漂亮。在北京我还认识了一个新朋友，他叫小海。他说，现在

中国人正在过春节，这是中国最重要的节日，跟我们的圣诞节一样重

要。他请我去他家，跟他的家人一起过春节。我跟他们一起看春节晚
jiārén

会，学包饺子，我特别有兴趣。这是我第一次在中国过春节。我觉得中
bāo

国的春节特别有意思，跟圣诞节不一样，跟新年也不一样，这是中国最

特别的节日。

祝你们春节快乐！

Sam

7月15日

Exercises

Match the English with the Chinese.

A 欢迎来中国　B 快要七点了　C 我的家人　D 第一次
E 开电视　F 看杂技　G 包饺子　H 精彩的节目

turn on the TV	welcome to China	it will be seven o'clock soon	make dumplings

my family members	watch acrobatics	first time	excellent programme

Listen 2

Listen to the recording and then choose the correct answer.

1）先＿＿＿＿电脑再上网。　　　　A 开　　　B 看

2）比赛＿＿＿＿＿开始了。　　　　A 早就　　B 快要

3）他们在表演＿＿＿＿＿。　　　　A 杂技　　B 京剧

4）这是你＿＿＿＿＿来中国？　　　A 第几次　B 第一次

5）我的＿＿＿＿对我很重要。　　　A 假期　　B 家人

Listen 3

Listen to the recording and then tick the correct box.

A	B	C	D	E	F
celebrates the New year with family at home	is watching the Spring Festival Gala on TV	says the film is starting soon	is watching it for the first time	will have a birthday party	thinks the acrobatics performance was brilliant

	A	B	C	D	E	F
小雨						
大卫						
大海						
京京						
玛丽						
丽丽						

Read 4

Complete the sentences according to the pictures.

1 ⬜ 我们一起＿＿＿＿。

2 ⬜ 杂技表演＿＿＿＿。

3 ⬜ 电视＿＿＿＿。

A 过春节　B 过圣诞节　　A 快要开始了 B 已经开始了　　A 开了　　B 没开

④ ____节目都很好看。

⑤ 现在这个画家的画特别____。

A 每个　　B 这个　　A 流行　　B 精彩

Read 5 *Read the following paragraph and answer the questions below in Chinese.*

　　每天晚上七点，妈妈都说："新闻快要开始了。"妈妈每天晚上都看电视新闻。她喜欢看新闻，还喜欢看晚会节目，她说晚会节目都很精彩，演员都很有名。爸爸也看电视，他看体育节目，他最喜欢看足球比赛。我喜欢上网，网上也能看电视节目。今年，网上也有一个新年晚会，他们说，这是第一次网络新年晚会。

Questions:

1) *What does Mum always say at seven o'clock?*

....

2) *What kind of programmes does Mum like to watch on TV?*

....

3) *What does Dad like to watch on TV?*

....

4) *What does the narrator like to do?*

....

5) *Is there something new happening this year? What is it?*

....

Talk 6 *Talk about how they are celebrating the Spring Festival in Chinese according to the pictures.*

①

②

③

④

Write 7 *Complete the sentences with the proper Chinese characters.*

1）晚会快要 ☐ ☐ （kāishǐ）了。

2）他是有名的 ☐ ☐ （zájì）技演员。

3）今天的节目很 ☐ ☐ （jīngcǎi），太好看了。

4）他是英国人，这是他第一 ☐ （cì）来中国。

Talk 8 *Look at the picture and answer the following questions in Chinese.*

1） *What's on TV in the morning and in the afternoon?*
2） *What time is it now?*
3） *What's on the TV next?*
4） *Do you like watching acrobatics?*

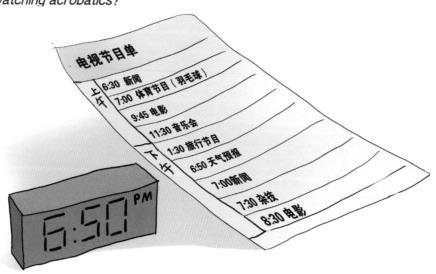

电视节目单

上午 | 6:30 新闻
7:00 体育节目（羽毛球）
9:45 电影
11:30 音乐会
下午 | 1:30 旅行节目
6:50 天气预报
7:00 新闻
7:30 杂技
8:30 电影

Write 9 *Write the following Chinese characters.*

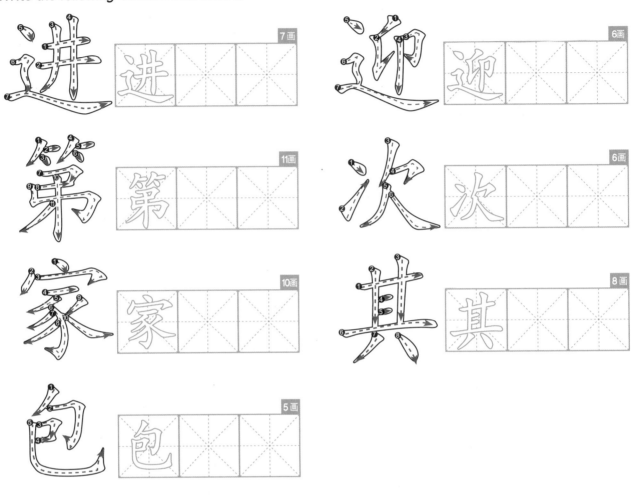

Read 10 *Phonetics.*

古诗(A Classical Poem)
Gǔshī

寻隐者不遇
Xún yǐnzhě bú yù

唐 · 贾岛
Táng · Jiǎ Dǎo

松下问童子，　言师采药去。
Sōng xià wèn tóngzǐ,　yán shī cǎi yào qù.

只在此山中，　云深不知处。
Zhǐ zài cǐ shān zhōng　yún shēn bù zhī chù.

第二十课 *Lesson* **20**

The New Mobile Phone Looks Really Good!
新手机真漂亮！

Learning Objectives

交际话题 Topic of conversation:

商品广告
Shāngpǐn guǎnggào
Product Advertisements

基本句型 Sentence patterns:

电视上有一个商品广告。

新手机真漂亮！

广告上说……

他的自行车跟我的一样。

New Words

1. 前天 qiántiān **n.** the day before yesterday
2. 商品 shāngpǐn **n.** commodity, good, product
3. 广告 guǎnggào **n.** advertisement
4. 手机 shǒujī **n.** mobile phone
5. 坏 huài **v.** to break down; to go bad
6. 旧 jiù **adj.** old
7. 辆 liàng **m.w.** (a measure word used for vehicles)
8. 礼物 lǐwù **n.** gift, present
9. 时尚 shíshàng **n./adj.** fashion; fashionable
10. 有点儿 yǒudiǎnr **adv.** some; a few; a little

Text

Part I

大海：京京，你看昨天的电视了吗？

京京：我昨天没看电视，前天看电
　　　　　qiántiān
　　　　视了。有什么好节目？

大海：电视上有一个商品广告。
　　　　　　　　　　shāngpǐn guǎnggào

京京：是新手机的广告吗？
　　　　　shǒujī

大海：你怎么知道？

京京：这些天的电视上常常有，

　　　　我也喜欢那个新手机。

大海：它真漂亮！

京京：广告上说，这是欧洲最新的、

　　　　最好的手机。

大海：哦，太喜欢了，我想买一个。

京京：你已经有一个手机了。

大海：我的手机坏了很久了，我要
　　　　　　　　huài
　　　　买一个新的。

京京：我也想买一个，我的手机太旧
　　　　　　　　　　　　　　　　jiù
　　　　了，可是新手机太贵了。

大海：我也觉得有点儿贵，可是它
　　　　　　　　yǒudiǎnr
　　　　很时尚！
　　　　　shíshàng

Part II

他的自行车跟我的一样

　　　每天我们在电视上看到很多广告，很多人看了广告就想买广告上的

商品。上星期我看到一个自行车的广告，我觉得那辆自行车真漂亮。我
　　　　　　　　　　　　　　　　　　　　　　　liàng

告诉了爸爸，爸爸就给我买了广告上的那辆自行车。他说，这是我的新年

礼物。我高兴极了。前天我骑新的自行车去学校了，看到大海也骑了一辆

lǐwù

新的自行车。他的自行车跟我的一样。大卫也骑了一辆新自行车，他的跟

我们的不一样。我们都很高兴，一起骑自行车去市中心了。

Exercises

Read 1 *Read the following words and expressions and then match them with the proper pictures.*

A 生日礼物　B 新自行车　C 昨天没有课　D 商品真多　E 今天过生日
F 电脑坏了　G 电影广告　H 一辆汽车　I 手机真贵　J 两个手机一样

Listen 2 *Listen to the recording and then choose the correct answer.*

1) _____我没看电视。　　　　A 昨天　　　B 前天

2) 电视上_____很多。　　　　A 节目　　　B 广告

3) 她的生日礼物是一_____自行车。　A 辆　　　　B 个

4) 你的新手机_____漂亮。　　　　A 真　　　　B 很

5) 这辆汽车_____了。　　　　　　A 快　　　　B 坏

6) 广告上说新_____快到了。　　　A 商品　　　B 手机

Listen
3
Listen to the recording and then tick the correct box.

A	B	C	D	E	F
had a lot of homework	belongs to Jingjing	is in the advertisement	it's the same as Dahai's	it's broken	new goods arrived

	A	B	C	D	E	F
手机						
自行车						
昨天我						
今天超市						
电脑						
电影						

Read
4
Complete the sentences according to the pictures.

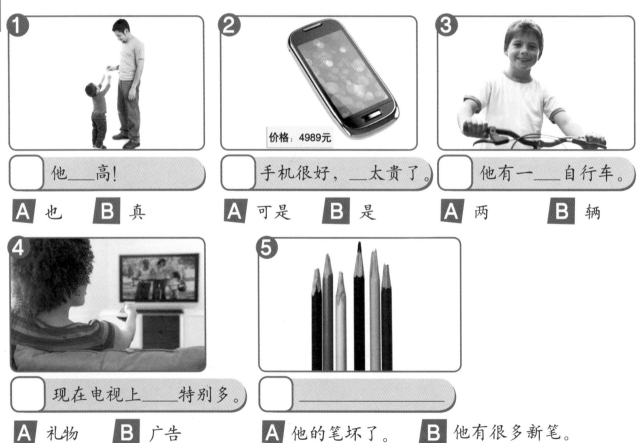

① 他___高!
　A 也　　B 真

② 手机很好，___太贵了。
　A 可是　　B 是

③ 他有一___自行车。
　A 两　　B 辆

④ 现在电视上___特别多。
　A 礼物　　B 广告

⑤ _____
　A 他的笔坏了。　　B 他有很多新笔。

Read 5

Read the following paragraph and answer the questions below in Chinese.

　　小雨喜欢看电视，她最喜欢看电视上的广告。她说，广告上的商品都很新、很漂亮。昨天的电视上有一个购物中心的广告，小雨特别喜欢。今天小雨第一次去了这个购物中心，她觉得这个购物中心真大、真漂亮，她希望每天都能来，可是这个购物中心离她家太远了。她还觉得这个购物中心跟她家旁边的超市不一样，商品很多，可是都太贵了。

Questions:

1)　Does Xiaoyu like watching TV?

....

2)　What kind of TV programmes does Xiaoyu like the most?

....

3)　What did Xiaoyu watch on TV yesterday?

....

4)　What does Xiaoyu like about the shopping centre?

....

5)　What does Xiaoyu think about the shopping centre compared to the supermarket near her home?

....

Read 6

Talk about the four posters in Chinese.

Write 7 *Complete the sentences with the proper Chinese characters.*

1）今天是1月3日，☐☐（qiántiān）是新年。

2）我的☐☐（shǒujī）跟他的一样。

3）你看今天的杂技节目了吗? ☐（zhēn）精彩!

4）电视上的☐☐（guǎnggào）特别多，我不喜欢。

5）圣诞节快要到了，我们买了很多圣诞☐☐（lǐwù）。

Talk 8 *Look at the pictures and answer the following questions in Chinese.*

1）　What did Mark see on the street?
2）　Can you describe the computers in the advertisement?
3）　What did Mark think he could do with a computer?
4）　What was the problem for Mark?
5）　What kind of computers do you like?

Write 9 Write the following Chinese characters.

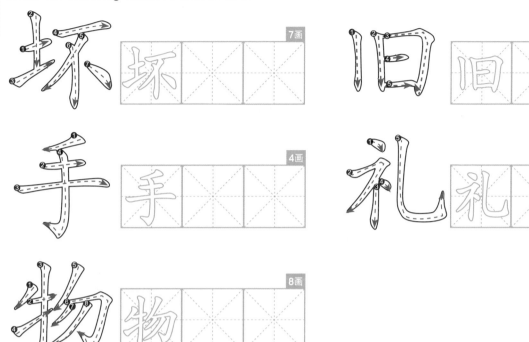

Read 10 Phonetics.

古诗(A Classical Poem)
Gǔshī

赋得古原草送别
Fù dé gǔ yuán cǎo sòngbié

唐 · 白居易
Táng · Bái Jūyì

离离原上草， 一岁一枯荣。
Lí lí yuán shàng cǎo， yí suì yì kū róng．

野火烧不尽， 春风吹又生。
Yě huǒ shāo bú jìn， chūnfēng chuī yòu shēng．

第二十一课 Lesson

21

Reading the Newspaper While Listening to Music
一边听音乐一边看报纸

Learning

交际话题 Topic of conversation:

阅读报刊
Yuèdú　bàokān
Reading Newspapers and Magazines

基本句型 Sentence patterns:

他天天都去图书馆。

我常常一边听音乐，一边看报纸。

哥哥在看杂志，姐姐在读书。

New Words

1. 差不多 chàbuduō **adj./adv.** similar, about the same; almost
2. 天天 tiāntiān **n.** every day
3. 报纸 bàozhǐ **n.** newspaper
4. 找 zhǎo **v.** to look for; to seek; to try to find
5. 资料 zīliào **n.** material

6. 一边…一边… yìbiān…yìbiān… **adv.** at the same time; simultaneously
7. 下班 xià bān **v.** to leave work
8. 上班 shàng bān **v.** to go to work
9. 做饭 zuò fàn **v.** to cook
10. 非洲 Fēizhōu **n.** Africa
11. 国家 guójiā **n.** country, nation, nation state

Text

Part I

（天天找丽丽的哥哥，他想打篮球。）

天天：丽丽，你哥哥在家吗？我们

一起去打篮球吧。

丽丽：哥哥不在家，他差不多天天
　　　chàbuduō tiāntiān

去图书馆看报纸，找资料，
　　　　　bàozhǐ　zhǎo zīliào

他在写一本书。

天天：你喜欢看报纸吗？

丽丽：喜欢，我每天都看报纸。你呢？

天天：我也喜欢，报纸上有很多新闻。

丽丽：我常常一边听音乐，一边看
　　　　　　　yìbiān　　　yìbiān

报纸。

天天：你现在能看中文报纸吗？

丽丽：还不能，我觉得看中文报

纸太难了。

天天：我觉得看英文报纸容易，

看法文报纸有点儿难。

丽丽：我有一本法文杂志，你想

看吗？

天天：当然想看，谢谢你。

Part II

哥哥在看杂志，姐姐在读书

我放学回家的时候，爸爸还没有下班。妈妈不上班，她正在做饭。妈
　　　　　　　　　　　　　　　　xià bān　　　　shàng bān　　　zuò fàn

妈天天都给我们做饭，有猪肉、牛肉、鸡、鸭，还有蔬菜和水果。她做的饭

很好吃。哥哥正在看杂志,他喜欢看体育杂志,他最喜欢足球杂志和网球杂志,他知道很多有名的运动员。姐姐在一边听音乐,一边看书,她喜欢看历史书和地理书。她常常去旅行,她去过亚洲、欧洲和非洲的很多国家。我回
Fēizhōu　guójiā
家先写作业。没有作业的时候,我喜欢看电视。电视上有很多节目,很有意思;可是也有很多广告,我不喜欢。

Exercises

Read 1 Match the English with the Chinese.

A 很多国家　　B 学做饭　　C 找资料　　D 买杂志　　E 放学了
F 一边吃一边看电视　G 她是非洲人　H 在看报纸　I 天天吃苹果　J 去上班

reading the newspaper	Class is over.	to search for information	

many countries	She is from Africa.	to buy magazines	to go to work

to learn to cook	to eat apples every day	eating while watching TV	

Listen 2 Listen to the recording and then choose the correct answer.

1）他_____都看电视。　　　　A 每天　　B 天天

2）这是英国最重要的_ _____。　　A 报纸　　B 节日

3）妈妈在家,她正在_____。　　A 做饭　　B 吃饭

4）我来的_____,他正在看电视。　A 时候　　B 星期

5）他们去过很多_____。　　　　A 地方　　B 国家

Listen
3
Listen to the recording and then tick the correct box.

A	B	C	D	E	F
sings every day	bought a music magazine	sang songs while doing homework	has been to three different countries	is cooking	can cook noodles

	A	B	C	D	E	F
爸爸						
大海						
小雨						
大卫						
丽丽						
玛丽						

Read
4
Complete the sentences according to the pictures.

①
＿＿手机都很漂亮。
A 个个　**B** 一个

②
我们人人都喜欢看＿＿＿。
A 明信片　**B** 杂志

③
这是今天的＿＿＿。
A 预报　**B** 报纸

④
爸爸回家的时候，我和妈妈、弟弟在＿＿。
A 做饭　**B** 吃饭

⑤

⑥

A 他一边骑自行车一边听音乐。

A 妈妈喜欢看历史书。

B 他骑自行车去音乐会。

B 妈妈做的饭很好吃。

Read 5 *Read the following paragraph and answer the questions below in Chinese.*

　　张老师天天早上坐公共汽车去学校，他喜欢一边坐车一边看报纸。今天早上，他买了报纸，还买了他喜欢的地理杂志。报纸上有他们学校的新闻，新闻上说，张老师的学校现在有很多新课程，学生们可以 (kěyǐ, can) 在学校学习，也可以在网上学习。因为可以上网学习，所以其他国家的学生也能学习他们的课程。张老师看了报纸特别高兴。

Questions:

1) What does Mr. Zhang go to school every day?

....

2) What does he like to do?

....

3) What did he buy this morning?

....

4) What's in the newspaper?

....

5) What does the newspaper say about Mr. Zhang's school?

....

6) How is Mr. Zhang feeling?

....

Talk
6

Talk about Ben's Saturday afternoon in the city square in Chinese according to the pictures.

Write
7

Complete the sentences with the proper Chinese characters.

1）今天的 ☐ ☐ (bàozhǐ) 上有我们学校的新闻。

2）他 ☐ ☐ (yìbiān) 吃饭 ☐ ☐ (yìbiān) 看电视。

3）他的 ☐ ☐ (guójiā) 在 ☐ ☐ (Fēizhōu)。

4）他的书架上有很多 ☐ ☐ (zázhì)。

5）他天天给我们 ☐ ☐ (zuò fàn)，他做的饭很好吃。

Talk
8
Look at the picture and answer the following questions in Chinese.

1） *What's the weather like?*
2） *What's Mark doing?*
3） *What's Sophie doing?*
4） *What are other boys and girls doing?*
5） *What is the couple doing?*

Write
9
Write the following Chinese characters.

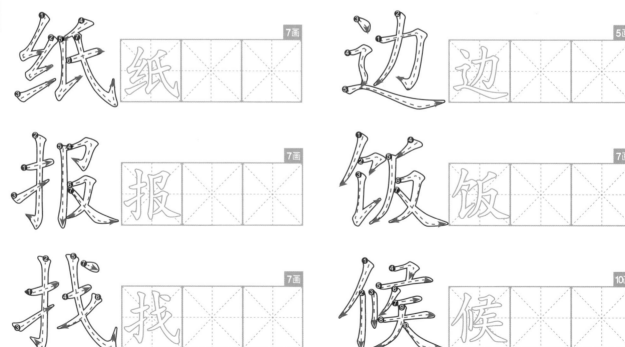

Read
10 *Phonetics.*

古诗(A Classical Poem)
Gǔshī

江雪
Jiāng Xuě

唐 · 柳宗元
Táng · Liǔ Zōngyuán

千山鸟飞绝，万径人踪灭。
Qiān shān niǎo fēi jué , wàn jìng rén zōng miè .

孤舟蓑笠翁，独钓寒江雪。
Gū zhōu suō lì wēng , dú diào hán jiāng xuě .

文化常识 Cultural Tip

中国的工艺美术

　　中国的工艺美术，历史悠久，不仅具有鲜明的民族风格和地方特色，而且制作精美，品种繁多，闻名于世。如北京的传统工艺品景泰蓝，浙江、江苏的丝绸，江苏的苏绣，陕西的剪纸，还有江西景德镇的瓷器等等，它们是世界各地游客在中国首选的纪念品。

Chinese arts and Crafts

Chinese arts and crafts have a long history, and with their distinctive ethnic characteristics, exquisite craftsmanship and rich varieties, they have attained great fame both in China and abroad. Typical representations of Chinese arts and crafts include traditional Beijing cloisonné, silk from Zhejiang and Jiangsu provinces, Suzhou embroidery, Shaanxi paper-cutting and Jingdezhen porcelain, etc. Chinese arts and crafts have become first choice souvenirs for visitors from all over the world.

第七单元小结　Unit Seven　Summary

1 主语+快要+开始+了！ Subject + is about to + start + auxiliary word 了！	春节晚会快要开始了！ The Spring Festival Gala is about to start! 新闻快要开始了！ The news is about to start!
2 每+量词+名词+都+很+形容词。 Every + measure word + noun + all + very + adjective.	每个节目都很好。 Every programme is amazing. 每个地方都很漂亮。 Every place is beautiful.
3 主语+特别+形容词。 Subject + (is) very + adjective.	杂技特别精彩。 The acrobatics are wonderful. 这个节目特别流行。 This programme is very popular.
4 名词+上+有+数词+量词+ 名词（词组）。 Noun + on (in)+ have + numeral + measure word + noun (noun phrase).	电视上有一个商品广告。 There is product advertisement on TV. 报纸上有一个香港的新闻。 There is news about Hong Kong in the newspaper.
5 主语+真+形容词！ Subject + really + adjective!	新手机真漂亮！ The new mobile phone is really attractive! 春节晚会真精彩！ The Spring Festival Gala is really amazing!
6 名词+上+说…… Noun + on (in) + say...	广告上说…… The advertisement says... 电视上说…… The TV says...
7 某人$_1$+的+名词+跟+某人$_2$+ 的+一样。 Sb.'s + noun + and + sb.$_2$ + the same.	他的自行车跟我的一样。 His bicycle is the same as mine. 大海的手机跟哥哥的一样。 Dahai's mobile phone is the same as his elder brother's.
8 某人+天天+都+动词+宾语。 Sb. + every day + all + verb + object.	他天天都去图书馆。 He goes to the library every day. 姐姐天天都骑自行车。 The elder sister rides a bicycle every day.

9 某人（＋常常）＋一边＋动词₁＋宾语₁，一边＋动词₂＋宾语₂。 Sb. (+ usually) + while + verb₁ + object₁, while + verb₂ +object₂.	我常常一边听音乐，一边看报纸。 I usually listen to music while I read the newspaper. 妈妈常常一边做饭，一边听新闻。 Mum usually cooks while she listens to the news.
10 某人＋在＋动词₁＋宾语₁，某人₂＋在＋动词₂＋宾语₂。 Sb. + be + verb₁ + object₁, sb.₂ + be + verb₂ + object₂.	哥哥在看杂志，姐姐在读书。 The elder brother is reading a magazine while the elder sister is reading books. 我在喝茶，弟弟在写作业。 I'm drinking tea while my younger brother is doing his homework.

第二十二课 Lesson

This Is My CV 这是我的个人简历 22

Learning Objectives

交际话题 Topic of conversation:

个人简历
Gèrén jiǎnlì
Curriculum Vitaes

基本句型 Sentence patterns:

你看见经理了吗?
这是我的个人简历。
字太小了，我看不清楚。

New Words

1 兼职 jiānzhí **n./v.** part-time job; to do a part-time job

2 服务员 fúwùyuán **n.** waiter/waitress

3 经理 jīnglǐ **n.** manager, director

4 看见 kànjiàn **v.** to see

5 个人 gèrén **adj.** personal, individual

6 简历 jiǎnlì **n.** CV

7 清楚 qīngchu **adj.** clear

8 当 dāng **v.** to act as; to take on the role of

9 图书管理员 túshū guǎnlǐyuán **n.** librarian

10 地址 dìzhǐ **n.** address

11 以前 yǐqián **prep.** before

12 经验 jīngyàn **n.** experience

Text

Part I

（天天在购物中心兼职，看见丽丽）

天天：丽丽，你来这里做什么？

丽丽：我来这里找兼职工作。你呢？
　　　jiānzhí
　　　你在这里做什么？

天天：我在这里做服务员，我已经工
　　　　　　　fúwùyuán
　　　作一个月了。

丽丽：怎么样？有意思吗？

天天：我觉得很好，很有意思。
　　　你也来这里工作吧。

丽丽：我先要找经理。
　　　　　　　jīnglǐ

天天：对。你看见经理了吗？
　　　　　kànjiàn

丽丽：没有，他不在。

天天：你有简历吗？
　　　　　jiǎnlì

丽丽：有。你看，这是我的个人简
　　　　　　　　　　　gèrén
　　　历。

天天：字太小了，我看不清楚。
　　　　　　　　　　qīngchu

丽丽：我回家再写一个，明天给你发
　　　电子邮件。请你帮我给经理，
　　　好吗？

天天：好。我看见经理的时候给他。
　　　希望你也能来这里兼职。

丽丽：太好了。

Part II

我写了个人简历

　　我是一个中学生。这个学期我的课不太多，我想当图书管理员，一边学
　　　　　　　　　　　　　　　　　　　　　　dāng　　　guǎnlǐyuán
习，一边工作。老师说，找兼职工作，要先写一个简历。我写了个人简历，

简历上有我的名字、电话号码、电子邮件地址，还介绍了我的课程、以前
　　　　　　　　　　　　　　　　　　　　dìzhǐ　　　　　　　　　　　　　　yǐqián

的工作和爱好。我在图书馆做过图书管理员，我有一些经验，我现在还想
　　　　　　　　　　　　　　túshū guǎnlǐyuán　　　　　　　jīngyàn

做这个兼职。今天我给图书馆的老师发了电子邮件，希望他们对我的简历

感兴趣。

Exercises

Read 1 *Match the English with the Chinese.*

A 看不见　　B 张经理　　C 我的简历　　D 发邮件　　E 没看见
F 兼职工作　G 作业不难　H 工作经验　　I 个人经验　J 在这里工作

work experience	send e-mails	Manager Zhang	the homework is not difficult	part-time job
didn't see	can't see	my CV	personal experience	work here

Listen 2 *Listen to the recording and then choose the correct answer.*

1）这是我们的_____。　　　　　A 经理　　　　B 简历

2）你_____张老师了吗?　　　　　A 看见　　　　B 看过

3）他每天都写_____。　　　　　　A 信　　　　　B 字

4）这是我们第一次来_____。　　　A 这里　　　　B 这个

5）他在购物中心_____。　　　　　A 工作　　　　B 兼职

6）他有在图书馆工作的_____。　　A 经验　　　　B 简历

Listen 3 *Listen to the recording and then tick the correct box.*

A	B	C	D	E	F
can't see the characters in the newspaper	has worked part-time in a supermarket	put his CV on the table	has been a manager	wants a part-time job	didn't include her e-mail address in the CV

	A	B	C	D	E	F
京京						
大海						
小雨						
大卫						
丽丽						
玛丽						

Read 4 *Complete the sentences according to the pictures.*

1

她不会___电子邮件。

A 读   B 发

2

这是我的_____。

A 个人简历   B 工作经验

3

在图书馆_____。

A 看书   B 兼职

4

_____。

A 我没看见经理。   B 我看见经理了。

5

报纸上的字太小了，_____。

A 他看不见   B 他没看见

Read
5

Read the following paragraph and answer the questions below in Chinese.

Josh打算一边学习，一边做兼职工作。他看见今天的报纸上有一个广告，广告上说，市中心的超市在找学生做兼职。Josh去了超市，可是他去的时候，经理不在。Josh给经理写了电子邮件，还给经理发了他的个人简历。经理很快给他发了电子邮件，经理说，他很高兴，因为Josh有兼职的经验，所以他明天就可以去超市工作。

Questions:

1) *What's Josh's plan?*

....

2) *What did he find in today's newspaper? What was it about?*

....

3) *What happened when Josh went to the supermarket?*

....

4) *What did Josh do then?*

....

5) *Did Josh receive a reply?*

....

6) *What did Josh get at last?*

....

Talk
6

Talk about Xiao Wang's schedule and his part-time jobs in Chinese according to the pictures.

Write 7 *Complete the sentences with the proper Chinese characters.*

1) 这是最大的超市，他在 ☐ ☐ (zhèli) 工作。

2) 他是学生，他想找一个 ☐ ☐ (jiānzhí) 工作。

3) 我不知道经理在哪儿，我没 ☐ ☐ (kànjiàn) 他。

4) 这是我的 ☐ ☐ ☐ ☐ (gèrén jiǎnlì)，您请看。

5) 这个电脑不能 ☐ (fā) 电子邮件。

6) 找工作的时候，兼职的 ☐ ☐ (jīngyàn) 很重要。

Talk 8 *Look at the pictures and answer the following questions in Chinese.*

1) What are the four people doing? What do they have in common?
2) How does Mark get his information?
3) How does Julie find her information?
4) Do you want to work part-time?
5) How do you find a part-time job?

Write 9 *Write the following Chinese characters.*

 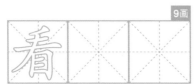 9画

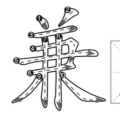 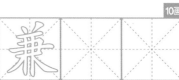 10画

  11画

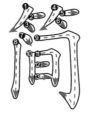 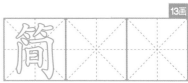 13画

  7画

  10画

 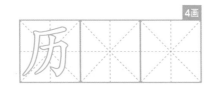 4画

 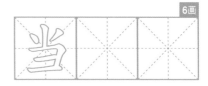 6画

Read 10 *Phonetics.*

古诗(A Classical Poem)
Gǔshī

凉州词
Liángzhōu cí

唐　·　王之涣
Táng　·　Wáng Zhīhuàn

黄河远上白云间，　一片孤城万仞山。
Huáng Hé yuǎn shàng báiyún jiān,　yí piàn gū chéng wàn rèn shān.

羌笛何须怨杨柳，　春风不度玉门关。
Qiāng dí hé xū yuàn yángliǔ,　Chūnfēng bú dù Yùménguān.

第二十三课 Lesson

23

Do You Have a Part-time Job?
你有兼职工作吗？

Learning Objectives

交际话题 Topic of conversation:

兼职计划
Jiānzhí jìhuà
Part-time Job plan

基本句型 Sentence patterns:

你还要写一个计划。

我替他写。

我想一边学习，一边兼职当记者。

New Words

1 有空 yǒu kòng　to have free time

2 事情 shìqing　n. thing

3 想法 xiǎngfǎ　n. idea, opinion

4 准备 zhǔnbèi　v. to prepare; to get ready

5 申请 shēnqǐng　v. to apply for

6 一定 yídìng　adv. certainly, definitely

7 报社 bàoshè　n. newspaper office

8 替 tì　prep. for; on behalf of

9 面试 miànshì　v. to interview

10 地点 dìdiǎn　n. place

11 礼堂 lǐtáng　n. assembly hall; auditorium

12 紧张 jǐnzhāng　adj. nervous

13 以后 yǐhòu　adv. afterwards, later

Text

Part I

（小雨、京京、大海三人见面）

大海：小雨、京京，你们现在有空吗？
　　　yǒu kòng

京京：有空，你有事情吗？
　　　　　shìqing

大海：是的。你们知道学校在找兼职
　　　学生吗？

京京：知道，我已经在学校图书馆
　　　兼职了。小雨，你呢？

小雨：我在体育馆兼职。

京京：大海，你呢？

大海：我没有，我也想找一个兼职工
　　　作。你们觉得我的想法怎么样？
　　　　　　　　　　xiǎngfǎ

京京：很好。你想做什么兼职工作？

大海：我想做记者。

京京：你准备简历了吗？
　　　zhǔnbèi

大海：准备了。

小雨：你申请当学校的记者，他们
　　　shēnqǐng
　　　一定对你的简历有兴趣，可
　　　yídìng
　　　是你还要写一个计划。

京京：什么计划？

大海：一个兼职计划，在学校报社
　　　　　　　　　　　　　bàoshè
　　　做记者的计划。

小雨：京京，你写过兼职计划吗？

京京：我写过，我替他写。
　　　　　　　　tì

Part II

一边学习，一边兼职当记者

很多学生都想做兼职工作，我也一样。我想一边学习，一边兼职当

记者。今天下午，想兼职当记者的学生都要面试，面试的地点是学校的
miànshì dìdiǎn

礼堂。我想有很多同学都会去面试。我有点儿紧张，我准备了个人简历，
lǐtáng jǐnzhāng

简历上有我的姓名、课程、考试成绩和工作经验。我还写了当记者以后的
yǐhòu

工作计划，这是京京和我一起准备的，我觉得这个计划准备得特别好，我

们计划了很多活动，我希望学校报社的老师和同学对我的计划有兴趣。

Exercises

Read 1 *Match the English with the Chinese.*

A 当记者　　B 替他写　　C 学习成绩　　D 第一次面试　E 没有申请
F 准备简历　G 学校礼堂　H 考试成绩　　I 不当画家　　J 比赛地点

to be a journalist	first interview	didn't apply	competition venue	to prepare a CV
exam result	to write for him	study performance	school auditorium	not want to be a painter

Listen 2 *Listen to the recording and then choose the correct answer.*

1) 他想_____老师。　　　　　　　A 当　　　　B 做

2) 他____我发了电子邮件。　　　　　A 给　　　　B 替

3) 我们都在这里_____。　　　　　A 面试　　　B 考试

4) 你们现在就去比赛_____吧。　　A 地方　　　B 地点

5) 请你们在_____里等我。　　　　A 礼堂　　　B 客厅

Listen 3 *Listen to the recording and then tick the correct box.*

A	B	C	D	E	F
was on the way to the auditorium	didn't go to the interview	wants to be a painter	has done well in the foreign language exam	hasn't prepared a CV yet	wrote a plan for someone else

	A	B	C	D	E	F
京京						
大海						
小雨						
大卫						
丽丽						
玛丽						

Read 4 *Complete the sentences according to the pictures.*

① 他想＿＿＿科学家。

Ａ 当　　Ｂ 是

② 这次考试不难，他的＿＿＿很好。

Ａ 作业　　Ｂ 成绩

③ 她＿＿＿我买东西。

Ａ 替　　Ｂ 请

④ ＿＿＿＿＿＿＿＿＿

Ａ 他们一边聊天儿一边准备晚饭。

Ｂ 他一边看电视，一边准备晚饭。

5 Read

Talk about Ben's interview in Chinese accprding to the pictures.

6 Talk

Read the following paragraph and answer the questions below in Chinese.

Josh很喜欢旅行，他去过很多地方。现在他想一边学习，一边兼职当导游（dǎoyóu, tour guide）。他在杂志上看见了一个广告，广告上说，一个旅行社下星期有一个面试，人们可以申请这个旅行社的兼职工作。想申请的人要准备个人简历。Josh对这个广告很感兴趣，他打算申请这个兼职工作，他要去面试。

Questions:

1) What does Josh like?

....

2) What does he want to do now?

....

3) What has caught his attention?

....

4) What is going to take place next week?

....

5) What should Josh prepare?

....

6) What is Josh going to do?

....

Write
7

Complete the sentences with the proper Chinese characters.

1）他想兼职 ☐ ☐ ☐ (dāng jìzhě)。

2）快要考试了，我们都在 ☐ ☐ (zhǔnbèi) 考试。

3）对这个工作感兴趣的人都可以 ☐ ☐ (shēnqǐng)。

4）我们在学校 ☐ ☐ (lǐtáng) 看表演。

5）这次的考试很重要，他很 ☐ ☐ (jǐnzhāng)。

Talk
8

Look at the pictures and answer the following questions in Chinese.

1） What is Mark doing?

2） What has Mark included in his CV?

3） What is David doing?

4） What does David want to include in his plan?

5） How would you prepare your CV, if you were to apply for a position?

6） What would be your plan for the new school magazine?

Write the following Chinese characters.

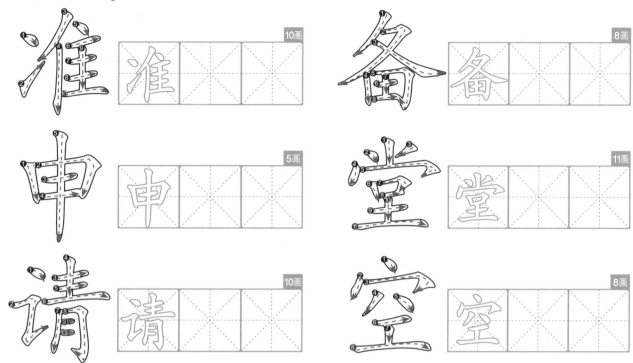

Phonetics.

古诗(A Classical Poem)
Gǔshī

九月九日忆山东兄弟
Jiǔ yuè jiǔ rì yì Shāndōng xiōngdì

唐 · 王维
Táng · Wáng Wéi

独在异乡为异客，　　每逢佳节倍思亲。
Dú zài yì xiāng wéi yì kè,　　měi féng jiājié bèi sī qīn.

遥知兄弟登高处，　　遍插茱萸少一人。
Yáo zhī xiōngdì dēng gāo chù,　　biàn chā zhūyú shǎo yì rén.

第二十四课 Lesson

24

What's Your Ideal Occupation?
你们的理想职业是什么？

Learning Objectives

交际话题 Topic of conversation:
理想的职业
Lǐxiǎng de zhíyè
Talking About Ideal Occupations

基本句型 Sentence patterns:
我的理想职业是……
现在理想的工作容易找吗?
做生意很难。

New Words

1 理想 lǐxiǎng **n./adj.** ideal

2 职业 zhíyè **n.** occupation, profession

3 生意 shēngyì **n.** business, trade

4 银行 yínháng **n.** bank

5 工资 gōngzī **n.** wages, salary

6 公司 gōngsī **n.** company

6 公司 gōngsī **n.** company

7 老板 lǎobǎn **n.** boss

8 校长 xiàozhǎng **n.** schoolmaster, principal

9 有的 yǒude **pron.** some

10 自己 zìjǐ **pron.** oneself

Text

Part I

（本、小雨、丽丽、大卫、天天、玛丽在一起聊天儿）

本： 你们理想的职业是什么？
lǐxiǎng zhíyè

丽丽： 我的理想职业是医生。

大卫： 我的理想是做生意，我想
shēngyì
去中国做生意。

天天： 做生意很难，我想在学校
工作，当法语老师。

玛丽： 我的理想职业是公司经理。
gōngsī

本： 你们觉得，现在理想的工作
容易找吗？

丽丽： 我觉得不容易。

大卫： 所以，我不要找工作，我要
自己当老板。
zìjǐ lǎobǎn

本： 小雨，你怎么想？

小雨： 我想将来当演员。

大卫： 当电影演员吗？

小雨： 不，我想当京剧演员，我很
喜欢京剧。

丽丽： 本，你呢？你的理想职业是
什么？

本： 我的理想跟你们的理想不一
样，我要当校长。

Part II

每个人的理想职业不一样

每个人都有自己的理想，每个人的理想职业也不一样，有的人想当老师，有
yǒude

的人想当科学家，有的人打算做生意，有的人将来要去银行，因为那里的工资
yínháng　　　　　　gōngzī

高；还有的人想当歌星、演员。我的理想职业是当记者，我觉得当记者最有意

思，能去很多地方，能认识很多人。我现在是中学生，我想一边学习，一边兼

职。我要申请当学校报社的记者，这不是很容易的事情。我准备了个人简历，

还写了一个计划。我很喜欢自己的计划，我希望老师对我的计划也感兴趣。

Exercises

Read 1 *Match the English with the Chinese.*

A 他的理想　　B 有的公司　　C 在银行　　D 做生意　　E 找工作
F 工资很高　　G 容易学　　H 有的人　　I 公司经理　　J 你自己

in a bank	to do business	yourself	easy to learn	someone
to look for a job	some companies	a high salary	manager of a company	his ideals

Listen 2 *Listen to the recording and then choose the correct answer.*

1）他打算＿＿＿＿＿＿。　　　　　A 做生意　　　　B 做经理

2）你理想的＿＿＿＿＿是什么？　　A 工作　　　　　B 职业

3）他们都在这个＿＿＿＿＿兼职。　A 银行　　　　　B 公司

4）工资高的工作＿＿＿＿＿。　　　A 不容易找　　　B 很难看见

5）你能＿＿＿＿＿写一个计划吗？　A 自己　　　　　B 替我

6）＿＿＿＿＿字太小了，我看不清。　A 这个　　　　　B 有的

Listen
3

Listen to the recording and then tick the correct box.

A	B	C	D	E	F
thinks it's not easy to find an ideal job	is working part-time at a film company	thinks the salary is low	ideal job would be working in a bank	wants to do business in the future	has some classmates who have gone travelling

	A	B	C	D	E	F
京京						
大海						
小雨						
大卫						
丽丽						
玛丽						

Read
4

Complete the sentences according to the pictures.

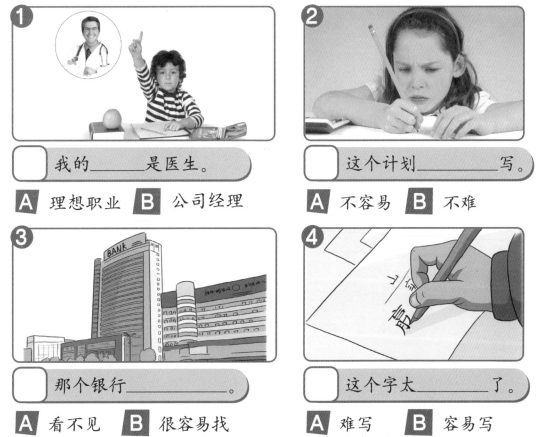

❶ 我的＿＿＿＿是医生。
A 理想职业   B 公司经理

❷ 这个计划＿＿＿＿写。
A 不容易   B 不难

❸ 那个银行＿＿＿＿。
A 看不见   B 很容易找

❹ 这个字太＿＿＿＿了。
A 难写   B 容易写

5

_____同学对做生意感兴趣。

A 有的　　**B** 没有

6

我喜欢_____。

A 一起去旅行　　**B** 自己去旅行

Read 5 *Read the following paragraph and answer the questions below in Chinese.*

　　每个人都有过很多理想，Vivian也一样。五岁的时候，她喜欢唱歌，她想当歌星；八岁的时候，她最喜欢上数学课和科学课，她想当科学家；十岁的时候，她和爸爸妈妈去中国旅行，她看了京剧表演，她想学京剧，要当京剧演员；十二岁的时候，她替哥哥在网上卖了一个手机，她觉得她将来可以做生意；现在Vivian十四岁，她在一个广告公司兼职，她觉得她的理想职业是记者。

Questions:

1)　What do all people have in common?

....

2)　What did Vivian want to be when she was five?

....

3)　What was her ideal profession when she was eight?

....

4)　What did she do when she was ten? What did she want to be then?

....

5)　What did she do when she was twelve?

....

6)　What's her ideal job now?

....

Talk
6
Talk about Millie's family and their jobs in Chinese according to the pictures.

Millie
哥哥
姐姐

Write
7
Complete the sentences with the proper Chinese characters.

1）他想在 ☐ ☐ (yínháng) 工作。

2）我想在这个 ☐ ☐ (gōngsī) 兼职，我给经理写了信。

3）我们都想找一个 ☐ ☐ (gōngzī) 高的工作。

4）A：你在找什么， ☐ ☐ (xiàozhǎng)？

　　B：我在找我 ☐ ☐ (zìjǐ) 的笔。

5）我觉得 ☐ ☐ (lǐxiǎng) 的工作不容易找。

Talk 8 *Look at the picture and answer the following questions in Chinese.*

1) *What does Mark see?*
2) *What is it about?*
3) *What do you think of the job offered?*
4) *Do you have any part-time work experience?*
5) *What's your ideal job?*

Write 9 Write the following Chinese characters.

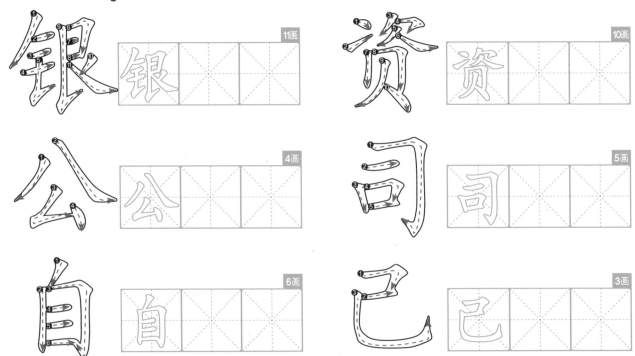

意 13画

Read 10 *Phonetics.*

古诗(A Classical Poem)
Gǔshī

春日
Chūn rì

南宋 · 朱熹
Nánsòng · Zhū Xī

胜日寻方泗水滨，无边光景一时新。
Shèng rì xún fāng Sìshuǐ bīn，   wúbiān guāngjǐng yìshí xīn.

等闲识得东风面，万紫千红总是春。
Děngxián shí dé dōng fēng miàn，wànzǐ-qiānhóng zǒngshì chūn.

元宵节和端午节

　　除了春节、中秋节，中国比较重要的传统节日还有元宵节、端午节等。

　　元宵节：农历正月十五，人们有吃元宵、看灯、猜灯谜的习俗，所以民间又称为"灯节"。

　　端午节：农历五月初五，这是一个很古老的节日。比较流行的说法是为纪念屈原而设立的节日，过此节时人们有吃粽子、赛龙舟等习俗。

The Lantern Festival and the Dragon Boat Festival

Besides the Spring Festival and Mid-Autumn Festival, the Lantern Festival and the Dragon Boat Festival are also important holidays in China.

The Lantern Festival is on the 15th day of the first lunar month. During this festival, people eat *yuanxiao* (sweet dumplings made of glutinous rice flour), and go out at night carrying paper lanterns with riddles written on them.

The Dragon Boat Festival is on the fifth day of the fifth lunar month and it is a festival with a long history. The most popular story about the origin of this festival is that it commemorates the poet Qu Yuan (340-278BC). On this day people hold dragon boat races and eat *zongzi* (glutinous rice stuffed with different fillings and wrapped in bamboo or reed leaves.)

第八单元小结	Unit Eight Summary

1 这/那+是+某人的+名词 (词组)。 This/that + is + sb.'s + noun (noun phrase).	这是我的个人简历。 This is my CV. 那是弟弟的中文作业。 That is the younger brother's Chinese homework.
2 主语+动词 (+宾语) +了+吗？ Subject + verb (+object) +auxiliary word 了 + interrogative word?	你看见经理了吗？ Have you seen the manager? 姐姐考试了吗？ Has the elder sister taken the exam?
3 主语+太+形容词+了，主语$_2$+ 动词+不+清楚/见。 Subject + very + adjective + auxiliary word 了, object$_2$ + verb + not + clearly/at all.	字太小了，我看不清楚。 I couldn't read it because the characters are too small. 声音太小了，他听不见。 He couldn't hear because the sound was too low.
4 某人+要+动词+宾语。 Sb. + is going to + verb + object.	他要写一个计划。 He is going to write a plan. 我要看中文电影。 I'm going to watch a Chinese film.
5 某人$_1$+替+某人$_2$+动词。 Sb. $_1$ + for + sb.$_2$ + verb.	我替他写。 I wrote it for him. 弟弟替她买。 The younger brother bought it for her.
6 某人+想+一边+动词+一边+ 动词 (+宾语)。 Sb. + want to + while + verb, while + verb (+object).	我想一边学习，一边当记者。 I want to study, and work as a journalist at the same time. 妹妹想一边学英文，一边做兼职。 The younger sister wants to learn English, while working a part-time job.
7 某人+的+理想职业+是+某职业。 Sb.'s + ideal occupation + is + a certain job.	我的理想职业是记者。 My ideal occupation would be to be journalist. 哥哥的理想职业是医生。 The elder brother's ideal occupation would be to be doctor.
8 主语+容易/难+动词+吗？ Subject + easy/difficult + verb + interrogative word 吗？	理想的工作容易找吗？ Is it difficult to find the ideal job? 那个汉字难写吗？ Is it difficult to write that Chinese character?
9 主语+很+容易/难+动词。 Subject + very + easy/difficult + verb.	做生意很难学。 It is difficult to learn how to do business. 今天的作业很容易做。 Today's homework is very easy to do.

Appendix: Vocabularies

A. Chinese-English Vocabulary List

生字词	拼音	词性	英文	页码
办法	bànfǎ	n.	way to handle affairs; method	86
帮/帮助	bāng/bāngzhù	v.	to help	62
棒球	bàngqiú	n.	baseball	86
包	bāo	v.	to wrap	144
报纸	bàozhǐ	n.	newspaper	158
北	běi	n.	north	25
比	bǐ	prep.	than; compared with	15
笔	bǐ	n.	pen	32
边	biān	n.	side	25
便宜	piányi	adj.	cheap	55
参加	cānjiā	v.	to join in; to take part in	134
草	cǎo	n.	grass, straw	110
草莓	cǎoméi	n.	strawberry	48
差不多	chàbuduō	adj./adv.	similar, about the same; almost	158
长	cháng	adj.	long	120
长城	Chángchéng	n.	the Great Wall	120
超市	chāoshì	n.	supermarket	48
成绩	chéngjì	n.	results, marks, achievements	79
城市	chéngshì	n.	city	120
除了	chúle	conj.	except, besides	127
厨房	chúfáng	n.	kitchen	25
窗户	chuānghu	n.	window	32
床	chuáng	n.	bed	32
春节	Chūn Jié	n.	the Spring Festival	127
春天	chūntiān	n.	spring	120
次	cì	m.w.	times	144
从	cóng	prep.	from	39
打	dǎ	v.	to make a phone call; to beat	96
蛋糕	dàngāo	n.	cake	48
当	dāng	v.	to act as; to take on the role of	168
当然	dāngrán	adv.	of course; sure	103
到	dào	v.	to get to; to arrive	39
德语	Déyǔ	n.	German	72
…的时候	…de shíhou	conj.	when …, at the time	127
地点	dìdiǎn	n.	place	175
地方	dìfang	n.	place	1
地理	dìlǐ	n..	geography	72

生字词	拼音	词性	英文	页码
地址	dìzhǐ	n.	address	168
第	dì	pref.	(prefix for ordinal numbers)	144
点心	diǎnxin	n.	light refreshments; desserts	48
电话	diànhuà	n.	telephone	1
电脑	diànnǎo	n.	computer	32
电影院	diànyǐngyuàn	n.	cinema	39
电子邮件	diànzǐ yóujiàn	n.	e-mail	8
订	dìng	v.	to book, to order	103
东	dōng	n.	east	25
东西	dōngxi	n.	thing, object	48
冬天	dōngtiān	n.	winter	120
队员	duìyuán	n.	member of a (sport) team	96
对不起	duìbuqǐ		I'm sorry; excuse me	134
对面	duìmiàn	n.	the opposite	25
多大	duō dà		how old	15
发	fā	v.	to send; to hand out	8
法语	Fǎyǔ	n.	French	15
放学	fàng xué		classes are over	72
非洲	Fēizhōu	n.	Africa	158
风景	fēngjǐng	n.	scenery	120
服务员	fúwùyuán	n.	waiter/waitress	168
附近	fùjìn	adv.	nearby; in the vicinity of	39
感冒	gǎnmào	n./v.	cold; to catch a cold	62
干净	gānjìng	adj.	clean	32
高	gāo	adj./n.	tall; (a person's) height	15
告诉	gàosù	v.	to tell	96
个人	gèrén	adj.	personal, individual	168
个子	gèzi	n.	height	15
给	gěi	v./prep.	to give, to let; to, for	8
跟	gēn	prep.	with, as	62
工资	gōngzī	n.	wages, salary	182
公司	gōngsī	n.	company	182
购物	gòu wù	v.	to go shopping	39
购物中心	gòuwù zhōngxīn	n.	shopping centre	39
故宫	Gùgōng	n.	the Forbidden City	120
故事	gùshi	n.	story	103
广场	guǎngchǎng	n.	square, plaza	39
广告	guǎnggào	n.	advertisement	151

生字词	拼音	词性	英文	页码
贵	guì	adj.	expensive	55
国家	guójiā	n.	country, nation, nation state	158
过	guò	v.	to cross; to go through; to experience; to live	110
过	guò	part.	(used after a verb to indicate a past action or state)	120
哈哈	hāhā	n.	(an exclamation used to express triumph or satisfaction)	120
还	hái	adv.	also, too; as well; in addition	48
汉语	Hànyǔ	n.	Chinese	15
汉字	Hànzì	n.	Chinese character	79
号码	hàomǎ	n.	number	1
河	hé	n.	river	110
黑	hēi	adj.	black, dark	110
花	huā	n.	flower	110
花园	huāyuán	n.	garden	32
滑雪	huá xuě	n.	skiing	134
画画儿	huà huàr	v.	to draw; to paint a picture	39
坏	huài	v.	to break down; to go bad	151
欢迎	huānyíng	v.	to welcome	144
回	huí	v.	to return	62
活动	huódòng	n.	activity	127
鸡	jī	n.	chicken	48
…极了	… jí le		extremely	96
计划	jìhuà	n./v.	plan; to plan	134
家人	jiārén	n.	family members	144
兼职	jiānzhí	n./v.	part-time job; to do a part-time job	168
简历	jiǎnlì	n.	CV	168
见面	jiàn miàn	v.	to meet	1
健康	jiànkāng	n./adj.	health; healthy, vigorous	86
角/毛	jiǎo/máo	n.	*jiao/mao* (a unit of Chinese money = ten cents, 1/10 of a yuan)	55
饺子	jiǎozi	n.	dumpling	127
觉得	juéde	v.	to think, to feel	86
教书	jiāo shū	v.	to teach	8
节日	jiérì	n.	festival	127
介绍	jièshào	v.	to introduce	8
斤	jīn	n.	*jin*(a unit in the Chinese weight system=1/2 kilogram)	55
今年	jīnnián	n.	this year	15
紧张	jǐnzhāng	adj.	nervous	175
进	jìn	v.	to come in	144
近	jìn	adj.	near	110

生字词	拼音	词性	英文	页码
京剧	jīngjù	n.	Beijing Opera	103
经理	jīnglǐ	n.	manager, director	168
经验	jīngyàn	n.	experience	168
精彩	jīngcǎi	adj.	brilliant, wonderful	144
久	jiǔ	adv.	for a long time	103
旧	jiù	adj.	old	151
就	jiù	adv.	exactly, precisely	25
剧院	jùyuàn	n.	theatre	103
开	kāi	v.	to turn on	144
开始	kāishǐ	v.	to begin, to start	72
看见	kànjiàn	v.	to see	168
考试	kǎoshì	n.	examination, test	79
科目	kēmù	n.	school subject	79
科学	kēxué	n.	science	72
咳嗽	késou	v.	to cough	62
可是	kěshì	conj.	but, however	103
客厅	kètīng	n.	living room	25
课程	kèchéng	n.	course, curriculum	79
快…了	kuài…le		soon; about to	120
快要	kuàiyào	adv.	soon; in no time	144
来	lái	v.	to come	48
来	lái	v.	(used before a verb to express an intention to do sth.)	86
老板	lǎobǎn	n.	boss	182
累	lèi	adj.	tired	96
礼堂	lǐtáng	n.	assembly hall; auditorium	175
礼物	lǐwù	n.	gift, present	151
里	lǐ	prep.	in, inside, among	32
理想	lǐxiǎng	n./adj.	ideal	182
历史	lìshǐ	n.	history	72
辆	liàng	m.w.	(a measure word used for for vehicles)	151
聊天儿	liáo tiānr	v.	to chat	8
溜冰	liū bīng	v./n.	to skate; ice skating	86
旅行社	lǚxíngshè	n.	travel agency	134
旅行团	lǚxíngtuán	n.	tour	134
买	mǎi	v.	to buy, to purchase	48
没关系	méi guānxi		it doesn't matter	134
门	mén	n.	door	32
面试	miànshì	v.	to interview	175

生字词	拼音	词性	英文	页码
名字	míngzi	n.	name	1
明信片	míngxìnpiàn	n.	postcard	120
那里	nàli	pron.	there; over there	39
南	nán	n.	south	25
南京	Nánjīng	n.	Nanjing	120
难	nán	adj.	difficult, hard	79
能	néng	v.	can; to be able to	62
胖	pàng	adj.	fat, obese	86
漂亮	piàoliang	adj.	beautiful	25
票	piào	n.	ticket	103
瓶	píng	m.w.	(a measure word used for bottles, jars)	55
其他	qítā	adj.	other	144
前天	qiántiān	n.	the day before yesterday	151
钱	qián	n.	money	55
清楚	qīngchu	adj.	clear	168
请	qǐng	v.	to invite	48
请假	qǐng jià		to ask for days off	62
庆祝	qìngzhù	v.	to celebrate	134
秋天	qiūtiān	n.	fall, autumn	120
去年	qùnián	n.	last year	15
热闹	rènao	adj.	busy, bustling	39
人们	rénmen	n.	people	127
人民币	rénmínbì	n.	renminbi (the currency of China)	55
认识	rènshi	v.	to know	8
容易	róngyì	adj.	easy	79
沙发	shāfā	n.	sofa	32
山	shān	n.	mountain	110
商品	shāngpǐn	n.	commodity, goods, product.	151
上	shàng	prep./v.	on; to go up; to serve	8
上班	shàng bān	v.	to go to work	158
上去	shàngqù	v.	to go up	110
少	shǎo	adj./adv.	few, less; seldom, hardly ever	86
申请	shēnqǐng	v.	to apply for	175
生病	shēng bìng	v.	to fall ill	62
生意	shēngyì	n.	business, trade	182
圣诞节	Shèngdàn Jié	n.	Christmas Day	134
时候	shíhou	conj.	when, during, while	96
时间	shíjiān	n.	time	96

生字词	拼音	词性	英文	页码
时间表	shíjiānbiǎo	n.	timetable, schedule	72
时尚	shíshàng	n./adj.	fashion; fashionable	151
市中心	shì zhōngxīn	n.	city centre; downtown	39
事情	shìqing	n.	thing	175
手机	shǒujī	n.	mobile phone	151
售票处	shòupiàochù	n.	ticket office	103
书架	shūjià	n.	bookshelf	32
树	shù	n.	tree	110
数学	shùxué	n.	mathematics	72
说	shuō	v.	to speak, to talk	15
岁	suì	n./m.w.	year of age; years old	15
所以	suǒyǐ	conj.	therefore; as a result	79
太	tài	adv.	too, extremely	55
特别	tèbié	adj.	special	103
疼	téng	adj.	aching, painful	62
踢	tī	v.	to kick, to play (football)	86
体育	tǐyù	n.	physical education	72
替	tì	prep.	for, on behalf of	175
天	tiān	n.	sky, weather, day	110
天天	tiāntiān	n.	every day	158
条	tiáo	mw.	(a measure word used for long narrow things like rivers, roads, etc.)	110
头	tóu	n.	head	62
图书管理员	tushū guǎnlǐyuán	n.	librarian	168
外语	wàiyǔ	n.	foreign language	15
晚	wǎn	n./adj.	evening, night; late	103
晚会	wǎnhuì	n.	evening party	127
王	Wáng	n.	(a surname)	1
为什么	wèishénme	adv.	why	96
卫生间	wèishēngjiān	n.	bathroom	25
问	wèn	v.	to ask	96
卧室	wòshì	n.	bedroom	25
舞龙	wǔ lóng		to perform a dragon dance	127
舞狮	wǔ shī		to perform a lion dance	127
西	xī	n.	west	25
希望	xīwàng	v./n.	to wish; wish	134
下	xià	adj./prep./v.	next; under, below; to go down	96
下班	xià bān	v.	to leave work	158
下来	xiàlái	v.	to come down	110

生字词	拼音	词性	英文	页码
夏天	xiàtiān	n.	summer	120
先生	xiānsheng	n.	mister, sir	1
想法	xiángfǎ	n.	idea, opinion	175
小时	xiǎoshí	n.	hour	96
小学	xiǎoxué	n.	primary school	8
校长	xiàozhǎng	n.	schoolmaster, principal	182
写	xiě	v.	to write	8
新	xīn	adj.	new	72
新年	xīnnián	n.	New Year; New Year's Day	134
新鲜	xīnxiān	adj.	fresh	55
信	xìn	n.	letter	8
星期	xīngqī	n.	week	134
姓	xìng	v.	to be surnamed; to be called by a surname	1
学期	xuéqī	n.	school term	72
学习	xuéxí	v.	to study, to learn	1
学校	xuéxiào	n.	school	8
鸭	yā	n.	duck	48
一边…一边…	yìbiān… yìbiān…	adv.	at the same time; simultaneously	158
一定	yídìng	adv.	certainly, definitely	175
一共	yígòng	adv.	altogether; in all	55
一些/些	yìxiē/xiē	adv.	some; a few	48
一样	yíyàng	adj.	the same	62
医院	yīyuàn	n.	hospital	62
已经	yǐjīng	adv.	already	134
以后	yǐhòu	adv.	afterwards, later	175
以前	yǐqián	prep.	before	168
椅子	yǐzi	n.	chair	32
因为	yīnwèi	conj.	because	79
银行	yínháng	n.	bank	182
英镑/镑	yīngbàng/bàng	n.	pound, sterling	55
英语	Yīngyǔ	n.	English	15
用	yòng	v.	to use	8
有的	yǒude	pron.	some	182
有点儿	yǒudiǎnr	adv.	some; a few; a little	151
有空	yǒu kòng		to have free time	175
有趣	yǒuqù	adj.	fun, interesting	72
有时候	yǒu shíhou	adv.	sometimes	39
羽毛球	yǔmáoqiú	n.	badminton	86

生字词	拼音	词性	英文	页码
元/块	yuán/kuài	n.	yuan/ *kuai* (a unit of Chinese money)	55
远	yuǎn	adj.	far	39
月饼	yuèbǐng	n.	moon cake	127
月亮	yuèliang	n.	moon	127
运动员	yùndòngyuán	n.	sportsman	96
杂技	zájì	n.	acrobatics	144
杂志	zázhì	n.	magazine	32
早	zǎo	n./adj.	morning; early	103
张	Zhāng	n./m.w.	(a surname; a measure word used for tickets, paper, and photos)	1
找	zhǎo	v.	to look for; to seek; to try to find	158
这里	zhèli	pron.	here	55
真	zhēn	adj./adv.	real; really	25
职业	zhíyè	n.	occupation, profession	182
中秋节	Zhōngqiū Jié	n.	the Mid-Autumn Festival	127
重要	zhòngyào	adj.	important	127
周	Zhōu	n.	(a surname)	1
猪肉	zhūròu	n.	pork	48
祝	zhù	v.	to bless, to wish	127
准备	zhǔnbèi	v.	to prepare; to get ready	175
桌子	zhuōzi	n.	table	32
资料	zīliào	n.	material	158
自己	zìjǐ	pron.	oneself	182
总是	zǒngshì	adv.	always	103
走路	zǒu lù	v.	to walk; to go on foot	86
昨天	zuótiān	n.	yesterday	79
作业	zuòyè	n.	homework	79
做饭	zuò fàn	v.	to cook	158

B. English-Chinese Vocabulary List

英文	生字词	拼音	词性	页码
(a measure word used for long narrow things like rivers, roads, etc.)	条	tiáo	m.w.	110
(an exclamation used to express triumph or satisfaction)	哈哈	hāhā	n.	120
(a measure word used for bottles, jars)	瓶	píng	m.w.	55
(a measure word used for for vehicles)	辆	liàng	m.w.	151
(a surname)	王	Wáng	n.	1
(a surname)	周	Zhōu	n.	1
(a surname; a measure word used for tickets, paper, and photos)	张	Zhāng	n./m.w.	1
aching, painful	疼	téng	adj.	62
acrobatics	杂技	zájì	n.	144
activity	活动	huódòng	n.	127
address	地址	dìzhǐ	n.	168
advertisement	广告	guǎnggào	n.	151
Africa	非洲	Fēizhōu	n.	158
afterwards, later	以后	yǐhòu	adv.	175
already	已经	yǐjīng	adv.	134
also, too; as well; in addition	还	hái	adv.	48
altogether; in all	一共	yígòng	adv.	55
always	总是	zǒngshì	adv.	103
assembly hall; auditorium	礼堂	lǐtáng	n.	175
at the same time; simultaneously	一边…一边…	yìbiān... yìbiān...	adv.	158
badminton	羽毛球	yǔmáoqiú	n.	86
bank	银行	yínháng	n.	182
baseball	棒球	bàngqiú	n.	86
bathroom	卫生间	wèishēngjiān	n.	25
beautiful	漂亮	piàoliang	adj.	25
because	因为	yīnwèi	conj.	79
bed	床	chuáng	n.	32
bedroom	卧室	wòshì	n.	25
before	以前	yǐqián	prep.	97
Beijing Opera	京剧	jīngjù	n.	48
black, dark	黑	hēi	adj.	138
bookshelf	书架	shūjià	n.	112
boss	老板	lǎobǎn	n	195

英文	生字词	拼音	词性	页码
bookshelf	书架	shūjià	n.	112
boss	老板	lǎobǎn	n.	195
brilliant, wonderful	精彩	jīngcǎi	adj.	150
business, trade	生意	shēngyì	n.	96
busy, bustling	热闹	rènao	adj.	185
but, however	可是	kěshì	conj.	178
cake	蛋糕	dàngāo	n.	29
can; to be able to	能	néng	v.	176
certainly, definitely	一定	yídìng	adv.	48
chair	椅子	yǐzi	n.	22
cheap	便宜	piányi	adj.	22
chicken	鸡	jī	n.	177
Chinese	汉语	Hànyǔ	n.	7
Chinese character	汉字	Hànzì	n.	167
Christmas Day	圣诞节	Shèngdàn Jié	n.	48
cinema	电影院	diànyǐngyuàn	n.	130
city	城市	chéngshì	n.	167
city centre; downtown	市中心	shì zhōngxīn	n.	39
classes are over	放学	fàng xué		22
clean	干净	gānjìng	adj.	72
clear	清楚	qīngchu	adj.	113
cold; to catch a cold	感冒	gǎnmào	n./v.	195
commodity, goods, product.	商品	shāngpǐn	n.	62
company	公司	gōngsī	n.	104
computer	电脑	diànnǎo	n.	162
country, nation, nation state	国家	guójiā	n.	80
course, curriculum	课程	kèchéng	n.	37
CV	简历	jiǎnlì	n.	55
difficult, hard	难	nán	adj.	194
door	门	mén	n.	2
duck	鸭	yā	n.	38
dumpling	饺子	jiǎozi	n.	38
east	东	dōng	n.	55
easy	容易	róngyì	adj.	62
e-mail	电子邮件	diànzǐ yóujiàn	n.	8
English	英语	Yīngyǔ	n.	15
evening party	晚会	wǎnhuì	n.	127
evening, night; late	晚	wǎn	n./adj.	103

英文	生字词	拼音	词性	页码
every day	天天	tiāntiān	n.	158
exactly, precisely	就	jiù	adv.	25
examination, test	考试	kǎoshì	n.	79
except, besides	除了	chúle	conj.	127
expensive	贵	guì	adj.	55
experience	经验	jīngyàn	n.	168
extremely	…极了	… jí le		96
fall, autumn	秋天	qiūtiān	n.	120
family members	家人	jiārén	n.	144
far	远	yuǎn	adj.	39
fashion; fashionable	时尚	shíshàng	n./adj.	151
fat, obese	胖	pàng	adj.	86
festival	节日	jiérì	n.	127
few, less; seldom, hardly ever	少	shǎo	adj./adv.	86
flower	花	huā	n.	110
for a long time	久	jiǔ	adv.	103
for, on behalf of	替	tì	prep.	175
foreign language	外语	wàiyǔ	n.	15
French	法语	Fǎyǔ	n.	15
fresh	新鲜	xīnxiān	adj.	55
from	从	cóng	prep.	39
fun, interesting	有趣	yǒuqù	adj.	72
garden	花园	huāyuán	n.	32
geography	地理	dìlǐ	n.	72
German	德语	Déyǔ	n.	72
gift, present	礼物	lǐwù	n.	151
grass, straw	草	cǎo	n.	110
head	头	tóu	n.	62
health; healthy, vigorous	健康	jiànkāng	n./adj.	86
height	个子	gèzi		15
here	这里	zhèli	pron.	55
history	历史	lìshǐ	n.	72
homework	作业	zuòyè	n.	79
hospital	医院	yīyuàn	n.	62
hour	小时	xiǎoshí	n.	96
how old	多大	duō dà		15
idea, opinion	想法	xiángfǎ	n.	175
ideal	理想	lǐxiǎng	n./adj.	182

英文	生字词	拼音	词性	页码
I'm sorry; excuse me	对不起	duìbuqǐ	v.	134
important	重要	zhòngyào	adj.	127
in, inside, among	里	lǐ	prep.	32
it doesn't matter	没关系	méi guānxi		134
jiao/mao (a unit of Chinese money = ten cents, 1/10 of a yuan)	角／毛	jiǎo/máo	n.	55
jìn(a unit in the Chinese weight system=1/2 kilogram)	斤	jīn	n.	55
kitchen	厨房	chúfáng	n.	25
last year	去年	qùnián	n.	15
letter	信	xìn	n.	8
librarian	图书管理员	tushū guǎnlǐyuán	n.	168
light refreshments; desserts	点心	diǎnxin	n.	48
living room	客厅	kètīng	n.	25
long	长	cháng	adj.	120
magazine	杂志	zázhì	n.	32
manager, director	经理	jīnglǐ	n.	168
material	资料	zīliào	n.	158
mathematics	数学	shùxué	n.	72
member of a (sport) team	队员	duìyuán	n.	96
mister, sir	先生	xiānsheng	n.	1
mobile phone	手机	shǒujī	n.	151
money	钱	qián	n.	55
moon	月亮	yuèliang	n.	127
moon cake	月饼	yuèbǐng	n.	127
morning; early	早	zǎo	n./adj.	103
mountain	山	shān	n.	110
name	名字	míngzi	n.	1
Nanjing	南京	Nánjīng	n.	120
near	近	jìn	adj.	110
nearby; in the vicinity of	附近	fùjìn	adv.	39
nervous	紧张	jǐnzhāng	adj.	175
new	新	xīn	adj.	72
New Year; New Year's Day	新年	xīnnián	n.	134
newspaper	报纸	bàozhǐ	n.	158
next; under, below; to go down	下	xià	adj./prep./v.	96
north	北	běi	n.	25
number	号码	hàomǎ	n.	1

英文	生字词	拼音	词性	页码
occupation, profession	职业	zhíyè	n.	182
of course; sure	当然	dāngrán	adv.	103
old	旧	jiù	adj.	151
on; to go up; to serve	上	shàng	prep./v.	8
oneself	自己	zìjǐ	pron.	182
other	其他	qítā	adj.	144
part-time job; to do a part-time job	兼职	jiānzhí	n./v.	168
pen	笔	bǐ	n.	32
people	人们	rénmen	n.	127
personal, individual	个人	gèrén	adj.	168
physical education	体育	tǐyù	n.	72
place	地方	dìfang	n.	1
place	地点	dìdiǎn	n.	175
plan; to plan	计划	jìhuà	n./v.	134
pork	猪肉	zhūròu	n.	48
postcard	明信片	míngxìnpiàn	n.	120
pound, sterling	英镑/镑	yīngbàng/bàng	n.	55
(prefix for ordinal numbers)	第	dì	pref.	144
primary school	小学	xiǎoxué	n.	8
real; really	真	zhēn	adj./adv.	25
renminbi (the currency of China)	人民币	rénmínbì	n.	55
results, marks, achievements	成绩	chéngjì	n.	79
river	河	hé	n.	110
scenery	风景	fēngjǐng	n.	120
school	学校	xuéxiào	n.	8
school subject	科目	kēmù	n.	79
school term	学期	xuéqī	n.	72
schoolmaster, principal	校长	xiàozhǎng	n.	182
science	科学	kēxué	n.	72
shopping centre	购物中心	gòuwù zhōngxīn	n.	39
side	边	biān	n.	25
similar, about the same; almost	差不多	chàbuduō	adj./adv.	158
skiing	滑雪	huá xuě	n.	134
sky, weather, day	天	tiān	n.	110
sofa	沙发	shāfā	n.	32
some	有的	yǒude	pron.	182
some; a few	一些/些	yìxiē/xiē	adv.	48
some; a few; a little	有点儿	yǒudiǎnr	adv.	151

英文	生字词	拼音	词性	页码
sometimes	有时候	yǒu shíhou	adv.	39
soon; about to	快…了	kuài...le		120
soon; in no time	快要	kuàiyào	adv.	144
south	南	nán	n.	25
special	特别	tèbié	adj.	103
sportsman	运动员	yùndòngyuán	n.	96
spring	春天	chūntiān	n.	120
square, plaza	广场	guǎngchǎng	n.	39
story	故事	gùshi	n.	103
strawberry	草莓	cǎoméi	n.	48
summer	夏天	xiàtiān	n.	120
supermarket	超市	chāoshì	n.	48
table	桌子	zhuōzi	n.	32
tall; (a person's) height	高	gāo	adj./n.	15
telephone	电话	diànhuà	n.	1
than; compared with	比	bǐ	prep.	15
the day before yesterday	前天	qiántiān	n.	151
the Forbidden City	故宫	Gùgōng	n.	120
the Great Wall	长城	Chángchéng	n.	120
the Mid-Autumn Festival	中秋节	Zhōngqiū Jié	n.	127
the same	一样	yíyàng	adj.	62
the Spring Festival	春节	Chūn Jié	n.	127
theatre	剧院	jùyuàn	n.	103
the opposite	对面	duìmiàn	n.	25
there; over there	那里	nàli	pron.	39
therefore; as a result	所以	suǒyǐ	conj.	79
thing	事情	shìqing	n.	175
thing, object	东西	dōngxi	n.	48
this year	今年	jīnnián	n.	15
ticket	票	piào	n.	103
ticket office	售票处	shòupiàochù	n.	103
time	时间	shíjiān	n.	96
times	次	cì	m.w.	144
timetable, schedule	时间表	shíjiānbiǎo	n.	72
tired	累	lèi	adj.	96
to act as; to take on the role of	当	dāng	v.	168
to apply for	申请	shēnqǐng	v.	175
to ask	问	wèn	v.	96

英文	生字词	拼音	词性	页码
to ask for days off	请假	qǐng jià		62
to be surnamed; to be called by a surname	姓	xìng	v.	1
to begin, to start	开始	kāishǐ	v.	72
to bless, to wish	祝	zhù	v.	127
to book, to order	订	dìng	v.	103
to break down; to go bad	坏	huài	v.	151
to buy, to purchase	买	mǎi	v.	48
to celebrate	庆祝	qìngzhù	v.	134
to chat	聊天儿	liáo tiānr	v.	8
to come	来	lái	v.	48
to come down	下来	xiàlái	v.	110
to come in	进	jìn	v.	144
to cook	做饭	zuò fàn	v.	158
to cough	咳嗽	késou	v.	62
to cross; to go through; to experience; to live	过	guò	v.	120
to draw; to paint a picture	画画儿	huà huàr		39
to fall ill	生病	shēng bìng		62
to get to; to arrive	到	dào	v.	39
to give, to let; to, for	给	gěi	v./prep.	8
to go shopping	购物	gòu wù	v.	39
to go to work	上班	shàng bān	v.	158
to go up	上去	shàngqù	v.	110
to have free time	有空	yǒu kòng		175
to help	帮/帮助	bāng/bāngzhù	v.	62
to introduce	介绍	jièshào	v.	8
to invite	请	qǐng	v.	48
to interview	面试	miànshì	v.	175
to join in; to take part in	参加	cānjiā	v.	134
to kick, to play (football)	踢	tī	v.	86
to know	认识	rènshi	v.	8
to leave work	下班	xià bān	v.	158
to look for; to seek; to try to find	找	zhǎo	v.	158
to make a phone call; to beat	打	dǎ	v.	96
to meet	见面	jiànmiàn	v.	1
to perform a dragon dance	舞龙	wǔ lóng		127
to perform a lion dance	舞狮	wǔ shī		127
to prepare; to get ready	准备	zhǔnbèi	v.	175
to return	回	huí	v.	62

英文	生字词	拼音	词性	页码
to see	看见	kànjiàn	v.	168
to send; to hand out	发	fā	v.	8
to skate; ice skating	溜冰	liū bīng	v./n.	86
to speak, to talk	说	shuō	v.	15
to study, to learn	学习	xuéxí	v.	1
to teach	教书	jiāo shū	v.	8
to tell	告诉	gàosù	v.	96
to think, to feel	觉得	juéde	v.	86
to turn on	开	kāi	v.	144
to use	用	yòng	v.	8
to walk; to go on foot	走路	zǒu lù	v.	86
to welcome	欢迎	huānyíng	v.	144
to wish; wish	希望	xīwàng	v./n.	134
to wrap	包	bāo	v	144
to write	写	xiě	v.	8
too, extremely	太	tài	adv.	55
tour	旅行团	lǚxíngtuán	n.	134
travel agency	旅行社	lǚxíngshè	n.	134
tree	树	shù	n.	110
(used after a verb to indicate a past action or state)	过	guò	part.	120
(used before a verb to express an intention to do sth.)	来	lái	v.	86
wages, salary	工资	gōngzī	n.	182
waiter/waitress	服务员	fúwùyuán	n.	168
way to handle affairs; method	办法	bànfǎ	n.	86
week	星期	xīngqī	n.	134
west	西	xī	n.	25
when, during, while	时候	shíhou	conj.	96
when…, at the time	…的时候	…de shíhou	conj.	127
why	为什么	wèishénme	adv.	96
window	窗户	chuānghu	n.	32
winter	冬天	dōngtiān	n.	120
with, as	跟	gēn	prep.	62
year of age; years old	岁	suì	m.w.	15
yesterday	昨天	zuótiān	n.	79
yuan/*kuai* (a unit of Chinese money)	元/块	yuán/kuài	n.	55